FLY FISHING
for TROUT
in MISSOURI

FLY FISHING for TROUT in MISSOURI

by

CHUCK TRYON

Drawings by Terry Martin
Maps and knots by Chuck Tryon

Edited by Chuck Tryon

OZARK MOUNTAIN FLY FISHERS

Printed in Marceline, Missouri, USA

Published by:

OZARK MOUNTAIN FLY FISHERS
1 Johnson Street
Rolla, Missouri 65401-3713

Front cover photo: Gary LaFontaine on the North Fork, by Chuck Tryon
Back cover photo: A wild Missouri rainbow, by Sharon Tryon

TABLE OF CONTENTS

PREFACE

WELL, FOLKS—here comes ol' Chuck one more time. Not as fancy as the first three times, perhaps, but still with all the detailed, hard-to-find-elsewhere information you've come to expect. A lot has changed in Missouri's fly-fishing-for-trout world since my last edition in 1999, and it's time to bring you up to date again.

What's changed? Where you can chase trout, for one thing. Some of the old places have increased public access now, and a couple of other old places have just plain disappeared.

Many of the trout-chasing rules have changed, too, all for the better. We've got some new catch-and-release water, new wild trout-management water, reduced creel limits and larger length limits to grow more trophy-size trout, and some new artificials-only areas, too. As fly fishers, that's good news for us all.

Trout- and fly-fishing organizations have changed, as well. A couple of the old clubs have disbanded, but new ones have risen to take their place. Organized fly fishers play a vital role in Missouri's trout-conservation efforts, and it's important for you to give them your support.

Literally hundreds of lesser, though still important, details also have changed. Where to stay and eat when you get there, telephone numbers to call ahead for lodging, campsite, canoe and guide reservations, e-mail addresses and other stuff.

The other thing that's changed is me. I passed the big six-six some time ago, and I've been chasing trout for well over half a century, now, almost forty years exclusively with flies. During that time, I've been through most of the stages attributed to this beloved sport, and have purposely tried to avoid some other stages I've read about or seen in others.

If all the years have taught me anything, it's that the rise and fall of western civilization does not depend on my and your fly-fishing prowess, and that it's easy to become an egomaniacal fly-fishing bore. So relax. Have fun. Enjoy. That's enough, and it's a lot.

The book you hold is as up-to-date as I knew how to make it. Read it, fold over some page corners in it, mark up the margins in it, dribble some coffee on it. Then throw it in your car and head for the water with it. That, after all, is what it's really for.

Chuck Tryon
Rolla, Missouri
January 30, 2005

ACKNOWLEDGEMENTS

AS WITH ANY ENDEAVOR of this sort, many folks made valuable contributions to its success. Some were in my life only briefly, others have been part of it seemingly forever. Some will understand my gratitude, others will be astonished to learn of it, modestly finding nothing extraordinary in their behavior to merit it. Some helped only with the first edition twenty years ago, but their information and influence carry on to this day. Others came along more recently. Here are just a few of those who helped so unselfishly and so much.

Michael McIntosh, Joel Vance, Tom Meade, and Steve and Sharon Wunderle, gifted outdoor writers who freely shared their knowledge of the journalistic craft with me.

Spence Turner, Mike Kruse and Terry Finger, capable trout biologists, and extraordinary fly fishers, as well.

Terry Martin, whose superb illustrations grace these pages of prose.

Linden Trial, Steve Jensen and Barry Poulton, my aquatic entomology experts who never refused cries for help.

Tom Shipley, Charlie Reading, Everett Chaney, Norm Hines, Parke Cory, Jim Rearrick and Don Wall, who shared much valuable knowledge with me that many others would have kept to themselves.

Sharon, my bride of 31 years; our daughter, Holly; and my dad, Phil, who first cast me on fly-fishing waters well over half a century ago.

And finally, Gary LaFontaine, Joan and Lee Wulff, Gardner Grant, Ted Shultz, Quint and Cicely Drennan, and Jackie Poehler, folks who've enriched my fly-fishing life in countless other ways that contributed directly to this epistle.

INTRODUCTION

THESE PAGES are the issue of a labor of love. Love for the trout, one of the Almighty's most splendid creations. Surely it was among the first to be conceived. Love for the soul-satisfying richness of the Ozark hills, with their icy springs and crystalline streams where the trout play out their role in the grand scheme of the universe. Love, too, for the many folks who nurture, protect and quest for this marvelous creature. Their companionship alone is ample reward for my efforts. And finally, love for the perception of life and man's place in it symbolized by the feathered illusion called the fly. No greater salve for body and soul has ever sprung from earthly hands.

To help share this love affair with you, I've sought the expertise of Show-Me State fisheries biologists, hydrologists, entomologists, streamwater chemists and others of a technical bent to offer you the best information available. I've also captured the savvy of notoriously successful Ozark trout stalkers to let you in on their streamside secrets. You'll find much here that appears nowhere else in fly- and trout-fishing literature.

Missouri's trout and their habitat need friends. Secret places are fun, but they have few protectors when trouble such as pollution and thoughtless land development threatens. I hope you'll renew your commitment to conservation, sportsmanship and high standards of streamside courtesy, not just because they're nice, but because they're necessary, both for the trout and for our continued enjoyment of them.

Please share my journey as we travel through not only the where-to and how-to, but also the why-to that enriches our lives so much.

WELCOME, NEIGHBOR

YUP.
The
rumors
are
true.
We've
got
some
mighty
fine
trout
fishing
here
in
Missouri,
and
we'd
love
to
share
it
with
you.
If
you're
unfamiliar
with
our
part
of
the
world,
here's
some
helpful
information.

The Ozark Wave

The farther you get off the interstate and into the hills, the more you're going to notice total strangers waving to you. Not big, arm-flailing waves, but little, laid-back, two-bent-finger waves through the windshield as you pass on the road. It's our way of saying "howdy, neighbor," and we invite you to give us a little, laid-back "howdy, neighbor" in return on your way past. Try it. It's fun.

The Biggest Myth in the Ozarks

You can argue this one with me all you want, but it's not going to change a thing. The biggest myth in the Ozarks is that, as long as you stay in the water, you can go anywhere you want. Sorry, all you believers—that's pure, self-serving baloney.

The truth is that avoiding trespass by staying in the water only applies to legally established navigable streams. On all other waters, you are legally allowed to be there only with the explicit permission of the landowners. That's no problem on publicly owned lands such as those managed by the Missouri Department of Conservation, Missouri Department of Natural Resources, U.S. Army Corps of Engineers, U.S. Forest Service, U.S. National Park Service, a couple cities and the James Foundation. Some private landowners benignly allow trespass out of the goodness of their hearts, but you'd better be sure before you try it.

Missouri's only legally established navigable trout streams are the Meramec, Current, Niangua, Eleven Point, White, North Fork of the White, James and Big Piney Rivers. That's all. Nuff said.

Fishing and Trout Permits

Obtain these necessities at the four trout parks, the clerk's office at any county courthouse, countless bait and tackle shops, any Wal-Mart store, and many fishing resorts and liveries. Permits are valid from March 1 to the end of February.

You can also get them from the Missouri Department of Conservation, PO Box 180, Jefferson City, MO 65102. On the Internet, look up MDC Permits. The phone number is (573)751-4115.

A resident annual fishing permit cost $12 in 2004, non-residents had to cough up $35. Daily fishing permits were $5.50. Trout permits cost $7.

Fly Availability

Unless you only use Wooly Worms, fur bugs or glo-balls, fly availability in outstate Missouri is limited. Outside the St. Louis and Kansas City metro areas, you can find fair to excellent fly selections at the Bass Pro Shop and Backcountry Outfitters in Springfield, the Clearwater Fly Shop in Columbia, Angling and Archery Outfitters and River Run Outfitters in Branson, Tim's Fly Shop near Roaring River State Park, the Roaring River Lodge gift shop, the Spring View Fly Shop, Reading's Fly Shop and Gaston's near Bennett Spring State Park, WindRush Farms Trout Stream near Cook Station, and at the Dogwood Canyon Orvis Shop. Unless you're planning to fish near these few places, my advice is to bring your favorite flies with you.

Guide Service

Full-time professional fly-fishing guides are scarce in Missouri, and tend to come and go quicker than a teenager's moods. Some canoe-rental services can guide you on our larger waters, but few will be able to offer any top-notch fly-fishing advice. The North Fork of the White River and Lake Taneycomo are exceptions, and I'll give you the details about them later.

The Weather

How you'll like our weather depends on what you're accustomed to. Late June, July, August and sometimes early September can be hot and sticky, with afternoon temperatures in the mid- to high nineties and humidities to match. We wet-wade or siesta during the worst of it.

Late September, October and November are a fly fisher's delight. Expect afternoon temperatures in the fifty-five to eighty-degree range and comfortable humidities.

December, January and February are a mixed bag. Come prepared for afternoon temperatures in the twenty- to forty-degree range, but don't be surprised if it gets into the low fifties, maybe even warmer. A few inches of snow fall every now and then, but it usually melts within a week. You folks from more northerly climates will love our ice-free rivers and year-round open trout season.

March, April, May and sometimes early June are the rainy season. March temperatures can vary from the thirties to the seventies, but warm weather gets more dependable from then on.

Things That Bite

Don't be intimidated by our things that bite. They're probably no worse here than where you're from, and a few things aren't nearly as bad.

For snakes, we offer rattlers, copperheads and cottonmouths. Most people fish for a lifetime without encountering the first. The other two are more common but seldom seen. Nowhere is any of them abundant. They're also protected by state law.

Harmless banded water snakes are fairly common, and you'll see them every now and then. Many locals call them "water moccasins," but they're not. Locals call the venomous kind "cottonmouths."

For spiders, we offer the black widow and brown recluse. The bites of both require immediate medical attention.

If we're really famous for anything in the biting category, it's probably for our chiggers and ticks. The first can make you scratch till your fingernails are red, but they're only an inconvenience. The others, of which we have ten species, come in three sizes. Seed

Poison ivy

ticks are the smallest (and often most ferocious), yearlings are a
little larger, and the adults are the largest. Each year, a few of
us get Rocky Mountain Spotted Fever from them, but you're more likely
to be struck by lightning or run over by a speeding beer truck.
Lyme disease and/or its lookalike(s) are also here, but very rare.
   Good news for many visitors is that mosquitos and biting flies are
no big deal here. They're seldom even a nuisance, and they'll never
drive you off the water as happens in some parts of the trout world.
   Oh, yeah. Also look out for our poison ivy and stinging nettle.
They can bite, too.
   There, now. That's not so bad, is it?

MISSOURI'S TROUT—WHERE ARE THEY?

TROUT were never native to the Show-Me State. The first to swim here
were brook trout stocked by the Missouri Fish Commission in 1879.
The first rainbows were stocked the following year. Browns came
along in 1893. Lake trout, salmon and grayling also were stocked in
those early years.

In most places, the fish perished because the waters were too warm.
In others, they managed to survive but failed to reproduce and
quickly disappeared when stocking ended. In about two dozen springfed streams, however, rainbow trout established self-sustaining populations.

The present trout resource consists of Lake Taneycomo, Bull Shoals
and Table Rock Lakes, a few small springfed ponds, and somewhere
between 200 and 400 miles of streams, depending on who you ask and
how you define trout water. The three big lakes, several of the
ponds and about 100 miles of streams are open to public fishing.
The other ponds and streams usually require permission from private
landowners for access.

A complete index of Missouri's major trout waters is at the end of
this book. For the public waters, I've described how to get there,
what the water's like, the kinds of trout there, where the nearest
lodging and campgrounds are, telephone numbers you may need, the
nearest restaurants and groceries, and a wealth of other useful information. I've been a little more secretive about the privately
owned waters, but some careful research will find them for you.

To whet your appetite, here's some introductory stuff. You can
look up the details later.

The Trout Parks

The best known of Missouri's waters are four trout parks—Bennett
Spring State Park near Lebanon, Maramec Spring Park near St. James,
Montauk State Park near Salem and Roaring River State Park near Cassville. There are a half-million fishing visits each year to these
parks, and the number continues to grow.

Two different seasons are available. The regular one runs from
March 1 to October 31, when lots of rainbows and an occasional brown
are stocked daily. Most weigh about three-quarters of a pound, but
there are always a few lunkers around, too.

With only two exceptions, the creel limit during the summer season
is four, and there's no length limit. Bennett Spring, Montauk and
Roaring River have stream reaches reserved for flies-only, Maramec
Spring doesn't.

The two exceptions are at Montauk and Roaring River. At Montauk,
several hundred feet of spring branch and three small lakes are managed strictly for catch-and-release fishing with flies only. Roaring River also has some catch-and-release water.

From the second Friday in November to the second Sunday in February, it's catch-and-release-only in all four trout parks. Winter-

season fishing is limited to Fridays, Saturdays and Sundays, and terminal tackle is limited to flies only.

A Missouri fishing permit and $3 daily trout tag are required for the summer season. The winter season requires a Missouri fishing permit and $7 special trout permit.

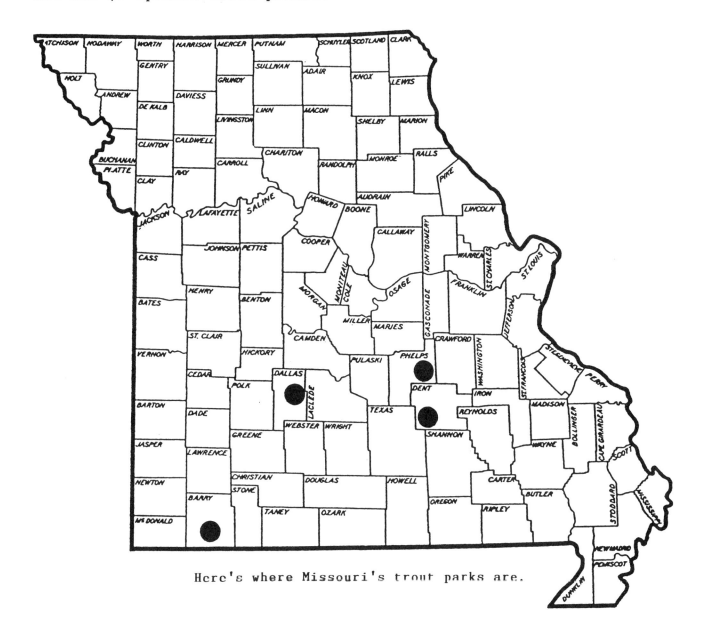

Here's where Missouri's trout parks are.

Blue Ribbon Waters

These are Missouri's premier trout waters. A few are stocked, most have streambred rainbow populations and are not. Two have brown trout.

Streams included here are the Current River above Cedargrove, the Eleven Point River above the Turner Mill Access, the North Fork of the

White River above Patrick Bridge, Crane Creek, Barren Fork Creek, Blue Springs Creek, Mill Creek, Spring Creek, and Little Piney Creek above the Milldam Hollow Access.

Terminal tackle is restricted to flies and artificial lures. The length limit is 18 inches for both rainbow and brown trout, and the daily creel limit is one. You'll need a trout permit to invite any home with you; you won't need a permit for just catching and releasing.

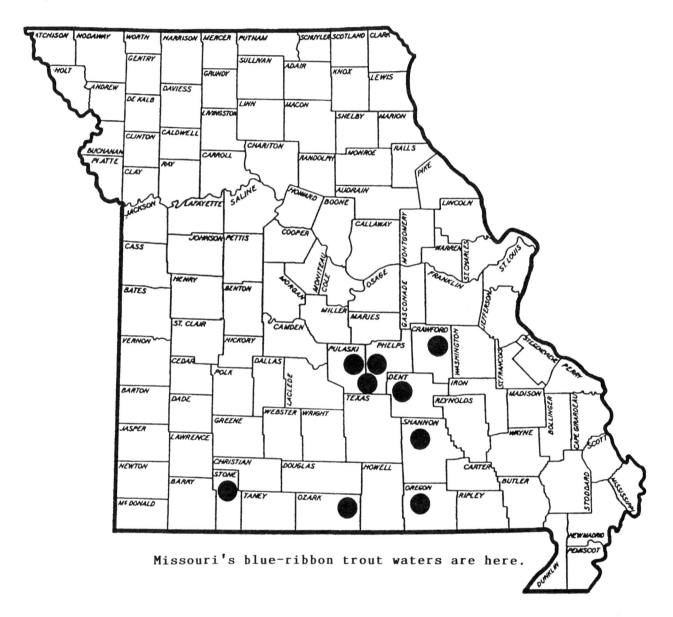

Missouri's blue-ribbon trout waters are here.

Red Ribbon Waters

These waters primarily hold stocked brown trout, but lesser numbers of rainbows also are present. The streams included here are the Meramec River, the North Fork of the White River below Patrick Bridge, and the lower $2\frac{1}{4}$ miles of Roubidoux Creek. Two fish 15 inches or longer can go in the creel. Terminal tackle is limited to flies and artificial lures in the Meramec River and Roubidoux Creek, but also includes natural baits in the North Fork. A trout permit is required only for creeling fish, not for catching and releasing.

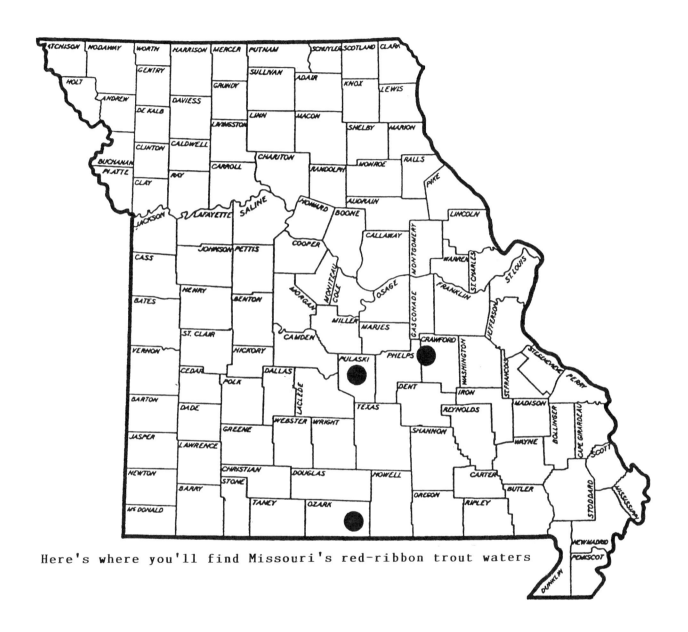

Here's where you'll find Missouri's red-ribbon trout waters

White Ribbon Waters

These waters are stocked primarily with rainbow trout and perhaps an occasional brown. The streams are Capps Creek, the Current River below Cedargrove, the Eleven Point River below the Turner Mill Access, Little Piney Creek below the Milldam Hollow Access, the Niangua River below Bennett Spring, Roaring River below the state park, Roubidoux

Creek for a ways below Roubidoux Spring, and Stone Mill Spring. And, even though it's not officially a trout-management area, I've also included the head end of Bull Shoals Lake below Powersite Dam near Forsyth in this category. You'll understand why when you get to the detailed writeup about it.

All types of flies, lures and bait are legal. Rainbow trout of any size may be kept, but brown trout must be 15 inches or longer to go in the creel. The daily creel limit is four.

Stone Mill Spring has a winter fish-for-fun season identical to that in the trout parks. All the other waters are open to catch-and-keep fishing year 'round.

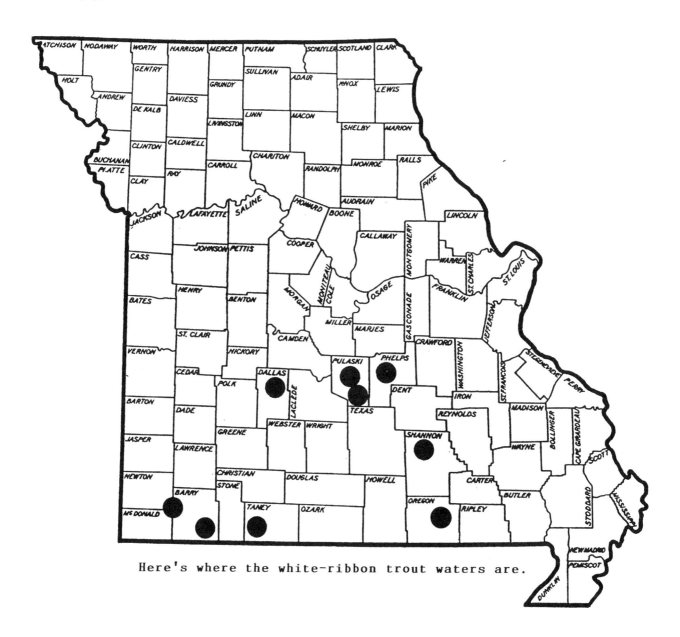

Here's where the white-ribbon trout waters are.

Urban Winter Trout Areas

From November through March, rainbow trout are stocked in a number of city- and county-park lakes in the St. Louis, Kansas City, Jackson, Jefferson City and Columbia metro areas. Most lakes are stocked every year, but a few come and go for who knows what reasons why. They all get too warm to support trout through the summer.

At most (but not all) of the lakes, all trout must be released from November 1 to January 31, and terminal tackle is restricted to flies and lures only. Thereafter, the creel limit is four trout of any size, and any kind of bait is okay. You'll need a state fishing permit, and a trout permit to creel any.

Additional cities are interested in this program. Keep your ear to the ground for news of a winter-trout lake coming to your area.

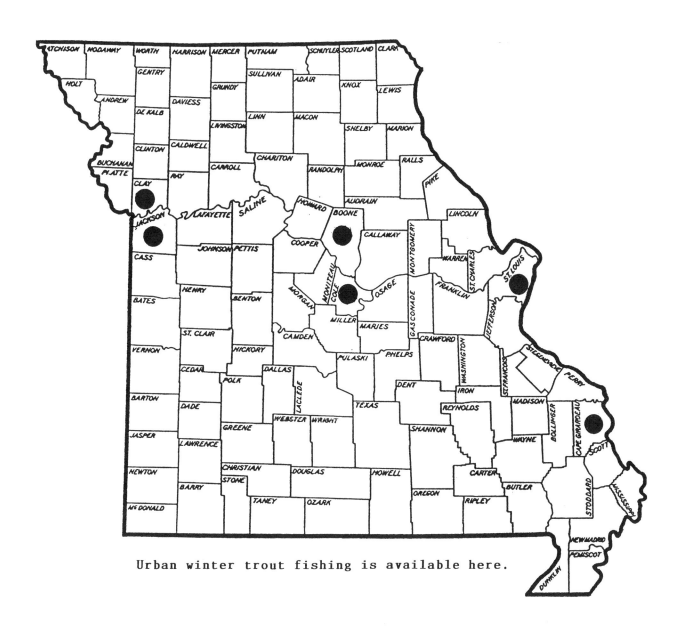

Urban winter trout fishing is available here.

Lake Taneycomo and Tributaries

Lake Taneycomo and its tributaries have their own unique regulations. Above the mouth of Fall Creek, rainbows from 12 to 20 inches long must be returned unharmed to the water. Rainbows smaller and larger may be creeled. Brown trout must be 20 inches or longer to be kept. The daily creel limit is four, of which only one may be a brown trout. Flies and artificial lures are legal; anything else is not.

Below the mouth of Fall Creek, rainbows of any size may be creeled, but browns still must be 20 inches or longer to go home with you. The daily creel limit is four, of which only one may be a brown trout.

All anglers fishing upstream of the Highway 65 bridge in Branson must possess a trout permit, regardless of whether they creel fish or not. Below Highway 65, a trout permit is required only if you're taking some home with you.

Table Rock and Bull Shoals Lakes

These two giant reservoirs in Barry, Stone, Taney and Ozark Counties were built by the Army Corps of Engineers for flood control, hydroelectric-power generation and recreation. Table Rock was stock-with trout briefly many years ago, but isn't any longer. A few trout wander into the lake from Roaring River, Dogwood Canyon, the Spring Valley Trout Ranch and the Beaver Lake tailwaters upstream in Arkansas, however, and Missouri bass anglers occasionally get surprised by a scarlet-striped "bass" on the end of their line.

Bull Shoals Lake, on the other hand, is heavily stocked with rainbow trout by the State of Arkansas. The fish don't care where the state line is, and Missouri anglers reap the benefit.

Except for the water close below Powersite Dam, there's little or no fly fishing for trout in Bull Shoals Lake itself. During the coldest part of winter, however, a few rainbows and a rare brown enter tributary streams. It's a fishery not many people know about, and you'll have to do most of your own scouting. Good places to start are Swan Creek at Forsyth and the old mill dam on Beaver Creek above Highway 160 near Kissee Mills.

You'll need a state permit, and a special trout permit to take any home. Rainbows of any size can be creeled, browns must be 15 inches or longer. The creel limit is four, and the season's open year 'round.

Commercial Fee-fishing Areas

Anglers willing to pay for a virtually guaranteed catch of large trout can visit a number of privately operated fee-fishing areas. Some have ponds, others have streams, some have both.

All these areas have rainbows averaging $1\frac{1}{4}$ pounds and ranging up to five pounds, occasionally more. A couple have golden rainbow

and/or brown trout. You must keep what you catch at most places, and
you pay for your catch by the pound. A few areas, however, also
offer catch-and-release fishing for a reasonable daily fee. No state
fishing permit or special trout permit are required. Some places are
open year-round, others close during the winter.

New operations appear from time to time, and old ones occasionally
vanish. Prices and rules change, too. If you're unsure where to go
or what you'll find when you get there, call or write ahead for
information.

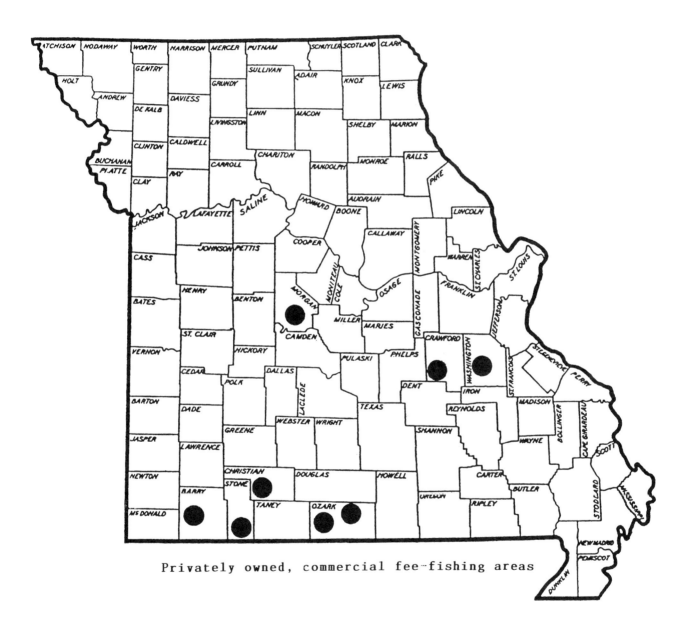

Privately owned, commercial fee-fishing areas

None of the Above

The rest of Missouri's trout waters are mostly privately owned or
accessible only through private land. You may get permission to fish

them occasionally, but don't be surprised if you're turned down. A number of streambred rainbow populations exist only because they're jealously protected by private landowners.

Several streams below private and federal hatcheries hold varying numbers of escapees. A number of small spring branches and springfed ponds are stocked by landowners for their own enjoyment.

You'll need a state fishing permit for these waters, and a special trout permit to creel any. The daily limit is four rainbows of any size, and the season's open all year long.

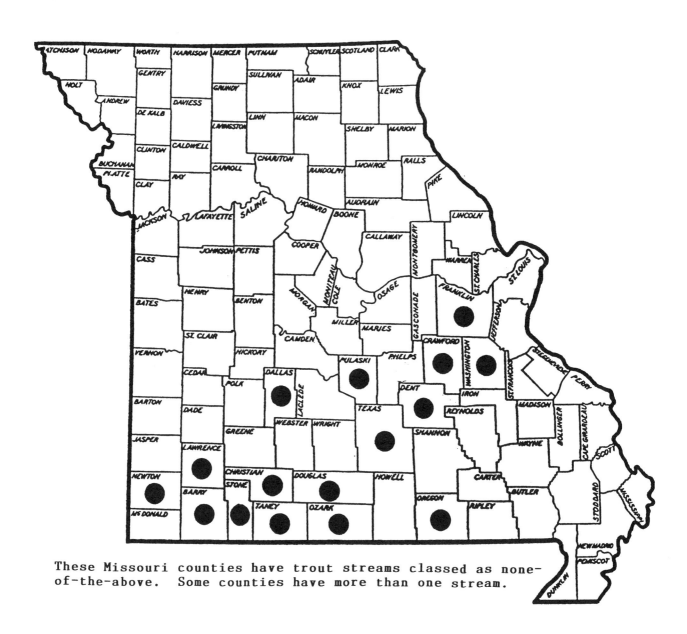

These Missouri counties have trout streams classed as none-of-the-above. Some counties have more than one stream.

WHY THE FLY ROD?

SOME OF THE GREATEST stories ever told are about fly fishers and
their quest. For the hopelessly smitten, the fly rod symbolizes a
way of life—a view of the world through special, rainbow-colored
glasses. For others, it's just plain fun. Almost no one starts
his fishing career with a fly rod, but hundreds of thousands end
there. How come?
  Philosophers and authors have pondered the question ever since
Dame Juliana Berners published <u>A</u> <u>Treatyse</u> <u>of</u> <u>Fysshying</u> <u>Wyth</u> <u>an</u> <u>Angle</u>
in 1496, a century and a half before Izaak Walton. Five-hundred
years later, no one has found the perfect answer.

To the pragmatic, the fly rod is an excellent tool for the capture of fish. It's the best at many times and places, beating casting and spinning rods hands down.

For the tired and troubled, the fly rod is massage and spiritual therapy. It works best in serene and beautiful places where life's meaning is uncluttered by material pursuits.

For the adventurous, the fly rod helps even the match between angler and prey. The delicate rod, gossamer leader and single hook help tilt the odds in the fish's favor, making victory all the sweeter.

To the inquisitive, the fly rod is a key to the mysteries of nature's aquatic treasure house. Pursued to its unreachable limit, no other angling method reveals so much about life's intertwined web—how the largest of creatures depend on the smallest and vice versa.

To the romantic, the fly rod is grace and beauty and the stuff of dreams. Casting is the delicate caress of the artist's brush, the trout's struggle an aquatic ballet, its capture like a sip of vintage wine.

The fly rod is all of these things and more. If it's yours, it can be anything you choose.

WHAT'S A FLY?

FLIES ARE LEGALLY DEFINED quite differently in Missouri than anywhere else in the world. Should you ever find yourself dealing with one of our Conservation Agents, the operative definition is, "An artificial lure constructed on a single-point hook, using any material except soft-plastic bait and natural and scented bait...that is tied, glued or otherwise permanently attached."

Most veteran fly fishers will immediately recognize this definition has little, if any, validity outside Missouri. Two- and three-point Atlantic Salmon flies are excluded, even though they've been counted as flies for hundreds of years. Countless casting plugs, even those foot-long, broom-handle musky lures, would be included if all but one hook point were snipped off, and soft-plastic legs are a common feature on some kinds of flies.

Fortunately, the only places Missouri's unusual fly definition is important are the fly fishing-only areas at Bennett Spring, Montauk and Roaring River, and at all four trout parks during the winter fish-for-fun (catch-and-release) season.

So, play by the rules in the trout parks, but leave them behind when you take your sport elsewhere.

ARE FLY FISHERS REALLY SNOBS?

A COUPLE of them are absolutely insufferable. There are a few others
the planet probably could spin quite nicely without, but that's true
of any crowd. Most fly fishers are the nicest folks you'll ever meet.
 So relax. Be proud of your fly-fishing skill, but don't treat
others like untouchables. The only contest is between you and the
fish, and the only person you have to impress is yourself.

LEARNING TO CAST

FIFTEEN OF THE SADDEST WORDS in the English language are, "I tried a
fly rod once, but I never could get the hang of it." Sound familiar?
  Some gentle probing always reveals the same story. "It looked like
fun, so I borrowed a rod and went down to the lake. Never could get
the fly past **my** feet. Lost a couple in the trees and got one in the

back of my neck. Finally said the heck with it—too complicated. Got my spinning rod out of the car and had a great time for the rest of the day."

Well, now. You didn't learn to drive a car by watching them pass on the street, and you didn't learn to cook by eating at McDonald's. Learning to cast with a fly rod is no different.

The single most important thing about learning to cast is to get good instruction. If you live where there's an organized fly- or trout-fishing club, you're in luck. All of them have members able and eager to lend you a hand. You'll find a list of clubs near the back of the book. New ones form and old ones vanish, so stay alert.

Some stores that specialize in fly-fishing equipment offer excellent instruction for a modest fee. If they don't, they're sure to know an expert who does. Don't be afraid to pay for good instruction. It's one of the best investments you'll ever make.

Most people learn from a fly-fishing friend. That's usually all right, but don't accept poor instruction just because it's from a friend.

Many husbands try to teach their wives. Sometimes it works, but usually it's a fiasco. Husbands, let your wife learn from someone else; let it be her decision instead of yours; and don't expect her to learn any faster than you did. It's one of the smartest moves you'll ever make, and the rewards are exquisite.

How can you tell if you're getting good instruction? Here are some things to look for:

Is your instructor holding the rod more than you are? He shouldn't be.

Is your instructor laying out long casts or fancy casts or otherwise showing off? He shouldn't be.

Does your instructor insist that you lock your elbow to your side and never move it? That style went out with the dinosaurs.

Does your instructor know anything except the roll cast? If not, find other help fast. Roll casting is never the best method except in tight spots where nothing else is possible.

Does your instructor recommend that you always use a float or bobber on your line or leader? If so, find someone else. It's the best method in only a few special situations. Most of the time you'll do better without one, once you learn how.

Most of all, don't give up. Even the experts crawled before they walked and walked before they ran.

CHOOSING THE RIGHT ROD

THE TYPE OF FISHING you intend to do should determine the kind of rod you choose. For small, brushy streams and unweighted or lightly weighted flies, a 7- or 7½-foot rod for a 4- or 5-weight line might be best. If you plan to comb big waters with heavy nymphs and streamers, a 9-foot rod for a 6- or 7-weight line would be better. The best all-around choice for Missouri trout fishing is an 8- to 9-foot rod for a 4- to 7-weight line.

Once you've decided on the rod length and line weight, let your budget be your guide. Most folks won't catch any more fish with an $800 rod than with a $50 one, and even a $20 rod is sometimes better than none at all.

There's an almost infinite variety of rods from which to choose. Fiberglass rods have fallen out of favor in recent years, but they're still pretty good. They combine durability and adequate performance with reasonable price. Whether you buy it or build it yourself, your best initial investment may be a medium-priced fiberglass rod.

Graphite rods are lighter in weight and more responsive to line and fly behavior than fiberglass, but you'll pay more for a good one. If you can't afford one now, plan for one in the future. Avoid bargain-basement graphite rods; many are poorly constructed and aren't the bargains they seem to be.

Split-bamboo (cane) rods are the sentimental favorite because of their long and rich tradition. In comparison to the other kinds, though, they're heavy, require a lot of care and usually are more expensive. Buy one only if you intend to have a love affair with it.

Besides the material it's made of, you also have some choices in your fly rod's flexibility—its action. A "fast-action" rod is the beginner's best choice. These are stiffer at the butt than at the tip. They lift the line off the water more effectively than rods which are equally flexible throughout their length. A fast-action rod is sometimes referred to as "stiff." A "slow-action" rod picks up line more slowly and is sometimes referred to as having "soft action."

Be sure to choose a rod with an adequate number of guides. Too few will cause the line to slap against the rod and thereby hamper casting. A good rule of thumb is to have at least one guide for each foot of rod length, and an extra one or two is even better. The first, or "stripper," guide should be about twenty inches from the rod grip.

Also be sure the ferrules connecting the rod sections fit snugly. On glass and graphite rods, a small amount of the ferrule's male fitting should remain visible after the sections have been connected. This allows the fitting to wear through time without becoming loose. Metal ferrules on bamboo rods, however, should seat completely.

Don't be fooled by rods which allegedly can be used for fly fishing, spinning or casting according to your choice of the moment. They may throw a jig or plug well enough, but they're often horrible for casting a fly. Cheap multi-sectioned "pack rods" are only a little better. Pay a bundle if you want a good one.

There's a persistent old myth that fly rods should have "proper" balance. Forget about balance. All that matters is whether or not the rod casts well and feels comfortable as you use it.

THE RIGHT LINE FOR THE ROD

A PROPERLY MATCHED rod and line makes casting a pleasure. Mismatched, they're an endless source of grief.

Most new rods have the proper line weight printed just forward of the grip. A few off-brand and many older ones don't, and the only way to match them up is to experiment with different lines until it feels right. Old-timers can often help if you're not sure what to look for.

Most lines are about twenty-five to thirty-five yards long. Line weight is determined by the weight of the terminal thirty feet. Commercially available fly lines range from 0-weight up to 15. The lightest ones are for stalking little brook trout in brush-infested rivulets. The heaviest are for saltwater fishing.

Fly lines come in different shapes, too. Level lines are the same diameter throughout their length. Once common, their popularity has faded because of their inferior casting properties. Their main advantage is low price.

Double-taper lines are thickest in the middle and taper toward both ends. They lift off the water easily and deliver the fly delicately. When one end becomes worn, you can turn them around and use the other. Double-taper lines are quite popular, especially for roll casting and dry-fly fishing.

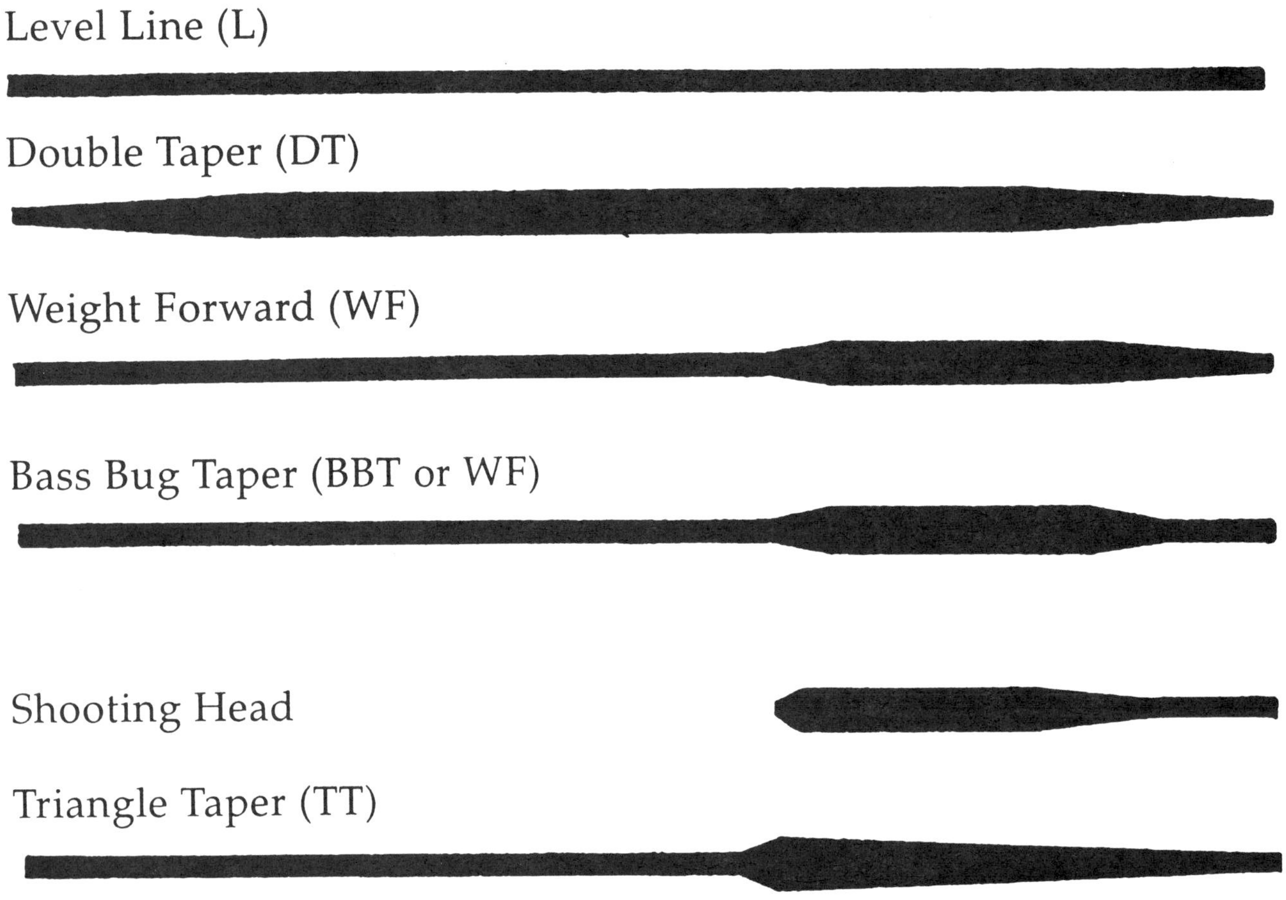

Level Line (L)

Double Taper (DT)

Weight Forward (WF)

Bass Bug Taper (BBT or WF)

Shooting Head

Triangle Taper (TT)

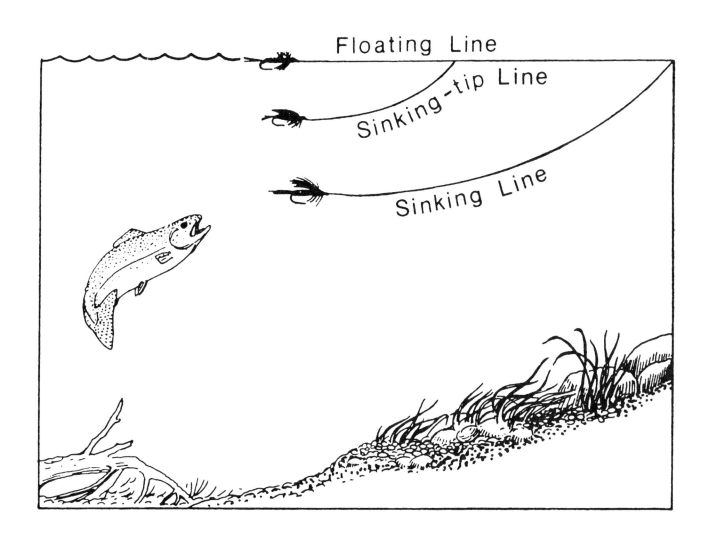

Weight-forward lines have a thick section up front which tapers to
a finer level section at the rear. They make long-distance casting
with heavy or big, wind-resistant flies much easier. They have the
disadvantage of landing on the water a little less delicately. If
you're a beginner, this is the line I'd recommend to learn with.

The bass-bug taper is a variation of the weight-forward line. Its
thick section tapers forward more steeply than the weight-forward
lines.

Shooting-taper lines are used for extreme long-distance casting.
They're essentially the heavy forward section of a weight-forward
line. Only thirty to fifty feet long, they're tied to a fine-diameter
level line or a long length of heavy monofilament. Their distance
advantage over weight-forward or bass-bug tapers is that the fine-
diameter running line behind the shooting-taper section speeds
through the guides with little friction. They're almost never used
on Missouri waters.

Triangle-taper line is a recent innovation that combines features
of weight-forward and double-taper lines. For long casting, triangle
tapers have the power advantage of the first and the delicacy of the
second.

Fly lines also are identified by the way they float or sink. Floating lines float throughout their length. If you're a beginner, you'll want to have one of these. They lift off the water easily and are suitable for all but the deepest pools.

Sinking-tip lines have a terminal section which sinks while the rest of the line floats. They're superb for fishing near the bottom of Missouri's larger trout streams. Learning to lift them free of the water for the backcast takes some practice, though.

Full-sinking lines sink throughout their length, and different types sink at different rates. They're excellent for lakes and other deep waters, but they're even more difficult to pick up for the backcast than sinking tips. They're seldom used for Missouri trout stalking.

Color is an important consideration in fly-line selection. You can choose from white to hot orange and almost anything in between. When afloat, they all look black from below.

For floating lines, I like ivory or light green for visibility. Others think hot pink or orange is more visible. Sinking lines and the terminal portion of sinking-tip lines generally are a less-conspicuous color, like dark green or brown.

When shopping for a fly line, you'll notice a series of letters and numbers on the box. They tell you almost everything you need to know about the line inside.

The first letter or two tells what the line taper is. L is for level, DT is for double-taper, WF is for weight-forward, BBT is for bass-bug taper, ST is for shooting-taper, and TT is for triangle taper.

The number which follows tells the line weight. The last letters tell whether it floats or sinks. F is for floating, F/S (floating/sinking) indicates a sinking-tip line, and S indicates a full-sinking line.

Thus, a fly line marked WF6F is a weight-forward, 6-weight floating line. What could be simpler?

One last thing. Many rods cast better with a line one weight heavier than what the rod is rated for. Check it out.

WHAT KIND OF REEL?

A FLY REEL serves dual purposes. It's a convenient place to store your line and one of your best friends when playing a fish. Be sure to choose one large enough to store your line plus a sufficient amount of backing. Unless you have a physical limitation in your arm or hand, avoid an automatic reel. They're heavy, don't store as much line and have more parts to break or malfunction.

Most experienced fly fishers prefer the single-action reel. You can pay up to several hundred dollars, but a good serviceable one can be bought for less than $40. If you're operating on a tight budget, scrimp on the price of the reel rather than on the rod or line.

Be sure extra spools are available for your reel. When you're ready to use several kinds of line, you'll only need extra spools instead of a whole new reel for each.

When shopping for a reel, be sure to check two things. If you're left-handed, make certain the reel can be reversed. Also, be sure the base will fit your rod's reel seat. Although most reels will fit most rods, a few won't.

BACKING

BACKING is a strong, fine-diameter, braided line attached to the reel at one end and the rear of the fly line at the other. When your dream-of-a-lifetime lunker heads downriver at ninety miles an hour, the backing gives you an extra length of leash to tame it.

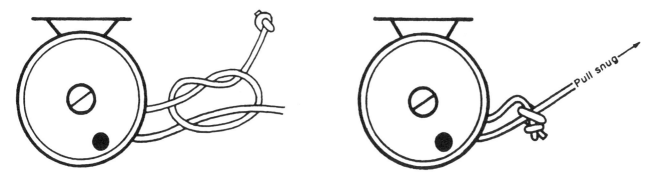

An Arbor knot is the usual way of attaching your backing to the reel.

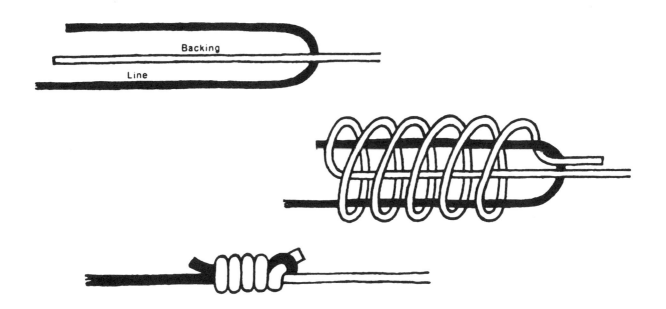

The Albright knot is the traditional way to connect your line and backing, but it's more difficult than some folks want to fool with.

To determine how much backing you'll need, wind your fly line on the reel. Then, wind on backing over the line until it's within about three-eighths of an inch of filling the reel. Snip off the backing at that point, and take both it and the line back off of the reel.

Tie the backing to the reel as shown in the illustration. Then, wind it evenly onto the spool by guiding it back and forth with your thumb and forefinger as you crank.

When you reach the end, attach it to the rear of the fly line with a commercially available Leader Link (made by Eagle Claw). Traditionally, the nail or Albright knot is used, but a Leader Link gives a smoother junction and is simpler by a mile.

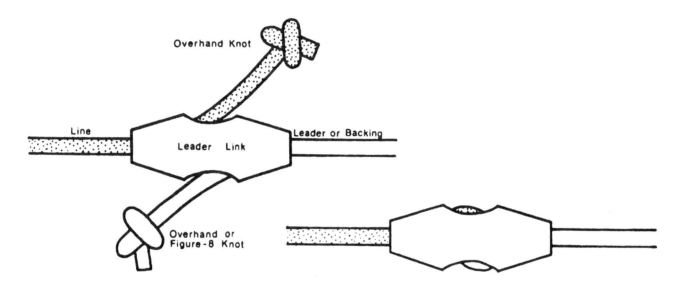

A Leader Link is the easiest and one of the smoothest ways to connect your line and backing. It's also a good, fast way to attach the leader to the other end of your line, even when your fingers are frozen. Be sure to make the knots large enough that they don't pull through the Leader Link ends.

LEADERS

A LEADER serves two purposes. To the fish, it's less conspicuous than your line. It's also much lighter in weight and lands on the water more delicately.

Leaders can be as short as two feet or as long as twelve, sometimes even more. Most commercially available leaders come in 7½- to 9-foot lengths. They're made of monofilament nylon and are perfectly adequate for most anglers.

Leaders are either tapered or level, just like lines. Tapered ones cast most effectively. Their diameter is largest at the butt where they attach to the line and smallest at the other end where they attach to the tippet or fly.

Some fly fishers enjoy tying their own tapered leaders with short sections of level leader material. There are all sorts of fancy formulae for how much material of a certain diameter should be tied in at each point along the leader's length.

Hand-tied tapered leaders may or may not cast more effectively than manufactured ones, but they have a major disadvantage in that the knots tend to collect algae as they drift. Manufactured tapered leaders are smooth throughout their length and don't have this problem. They're entirely adequate for most anglers.

When shopping for leader, check the in-formation on the pack-

SPENCER
FINE LEADERS

Tapered
Nylon
Leaders

Model	Size	Tip Dia.	Butt Dia.	Test
OO	7½–2X	.009"	.018"	4 lb.

MFD. BY SPENCER & Coho Pond Co. 53806
MADE IN U.S.A.

age. The length is given in feet, and the tip and butt diameters are given in inches. The leader's strength is indicated by its "test" which is the maximum weight it can lift without breaking.

The other bit of information on the package is a little more mysterious than the rest. It's the X rating. Fly fishers love to talk (and lie) about the X rating of their leaders and tippets.

X is just another way of describing the leader's smallest diameter. To decipher the system, remember the Rule of Eleven—the X and the diameter, expressed in thousandths of an inch, always add up to eleven. For example, 2X leader has a minimum diameter of .009 inch, and 7X leader has a minimum diameter of .004 inch.

Obviously, leaders with small X ratings are stronger than those with with large ones, and vice versa. Any tall tale about the conquest of a monster trout should always include the X rating of the leader or tippet it was caught on. When angling around the pot-bellied stove, the largest trout are almost invariably subdued with the most gos-samer leader. In actuality, however, most trout fishing is done with 3X to 6X leaders.

TIPPET

A TIPPET is a section of level monofilament attached to the tip of the leader. The fly is tied to the tippet. The tippet usually is two to four feet long, but can be longer.

A tippet serves at least three purposes. It's more slender than the leader and less conspicuous to the fish. It cuts down on the expense of leader replacement. Instead of cutting the more expensive leader back each time you tie on a new fly, you just keep trimming the tippet instead. Finally, it's usually more flexible than the leader, allowing your fly to drift more naturally.

Tippet material is described by its diameter, X rating and test strength, just like leader. It's also lied about, just like leader.

KNOTS

KNOTS are essential to the fly-fishing craft. Some people make a science of them, and that's good. Others use the first knot they ever learned, and would sooner change their politics or religion. That's bad. Knots have improved a lot over the years, and there are many good ones. Entire books have been written about nothing else. I can't tell you everything there is to know, but here's enough to get you started.

I've already explained how to tie your line or backing to the reel, and I've suggested using a Leader Link to connect the backing to the rear end of your line. All that's left is to connect the leader to your line, the tippet to your leader and the fly to your tippet.

There are several ways to connect the leader to the line, and everyone has their favorite. The simplest, which is quite adequate for most people, is to use a Leader Link. More traditional folks use the nail knot. If you want to be fancy, use the nail-knot variation cal-

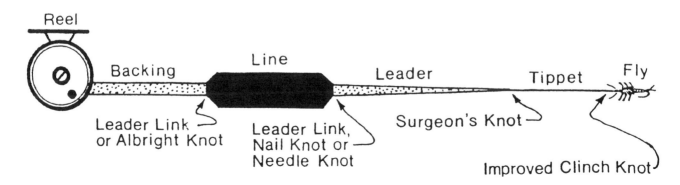

led the needle knot. A dab of epoxy on the knot will smooth it over, making it less apt to snag in the tip guide.

Use the surgeon's knot to tie the tippet to the leader. Some ol' timers may try to talk you into using a blood knot instead, but don't let 'em. The surgeon's knot is stronger and simpler by a mile.

To attach the fly to the tippet, use the improved clinch knot. Several other knots are just as good, but none are better, and this one's the simplest.

Tightening any knot slowly instead of rapidly helps retain the monofilament's and knot's strength. Dipping the loosely tied knot in the water for several seconds before tightening it also helps. Spitting on it is a poor substitute for dipping it in the water.

One knot in particular is the fly-caster's nemesis. Affectionately known as the wind knot, it's a simple overhand that mysteriously appears, sometimes in duplicate or triplicate, in your leader or tippet after a session of casting. Alleged to be caused by the wind, wind knots actually are a sign of imperfect casting. They're best avoided because they weaken your connection to your quarry. If they appear in spite of your best efforts, replace the knotted section with new material.

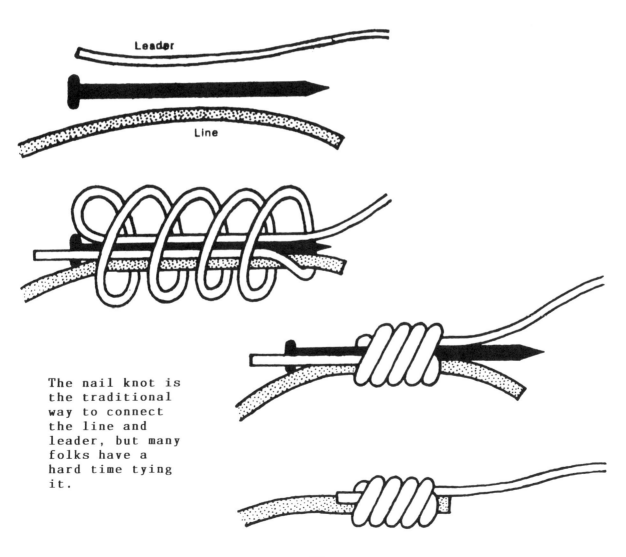

The nail knot is the traditional way to connect the line and leader, but many folks have a hard time tying it.

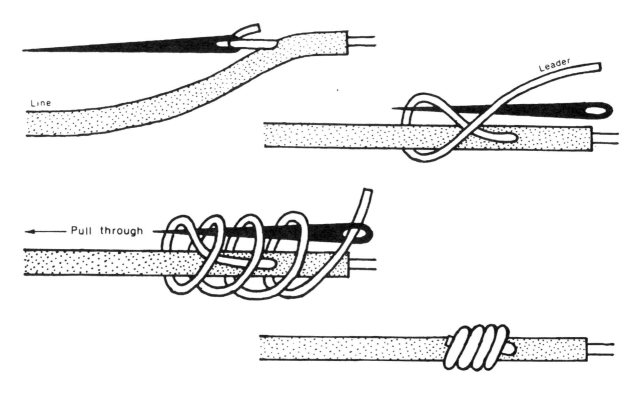

The needle knot is a smoother variation of the nail knot.
A dap of epoxy over the knot will make it even smoother
and less likely to catch in the tip guide.

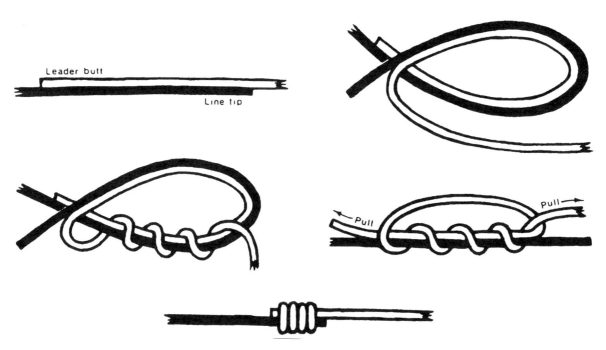

The Uni-knot splice is a quick and simple way to connect
your line and leader, especially when your fingers are frozen.

When first learning new knots, practice with clothesline rope or some other heavy cord. Use a large eye screw in a board for the hook. You can go to the much smaller, real thing after you've got the moves down right.

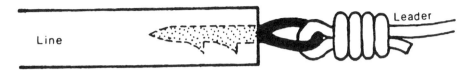

These little eyelets on a barbed shaft provide the smoothest of all line-to-leader junctions. Unfortunately, they're the dickens to get in right, they may fray the end of your line after a while, and they break the taper continuity of your line and leader.

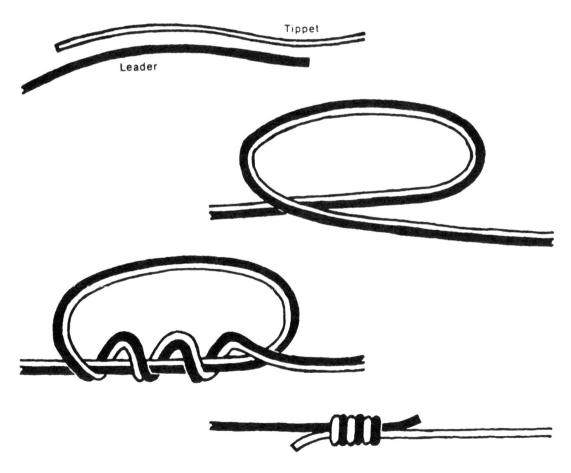

The surgeon's knot is the simplest, fastest and strongest way to connect your leader and tippet.

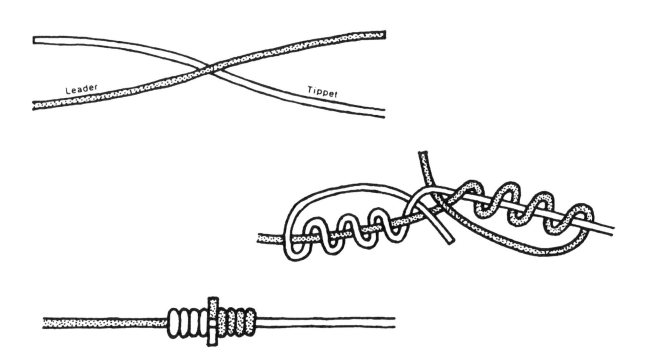

The blood knot is the traditional way to connect your leader and tippet, but only an architectural genius can tie it, especially with cold fingers.

The clinch knot (top) probably is the most common way to attach the fly to the tippet. It's fast and simple, but those are its only virtues. The improved clinch knot (bottom) is vastly better.

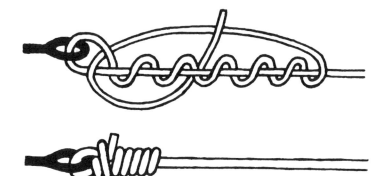

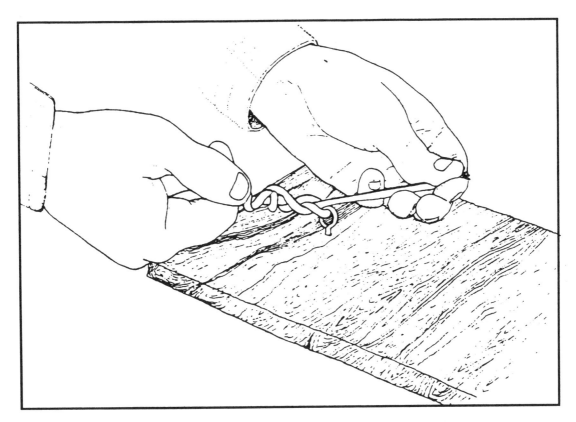

Trying to learn new fly-to-tippet knots can be frustrating
because of the small materials you're working with. It's
easier to use a piece of stout cord and a large eye screw
in a board to figure out the right moves before trying the
real thing.

WADERS

KNOWN to the more jocular as "rubber pants," they come in two styles
—boot-foot and stocking-foot. The boot-foot kind is most common. It
has the boot or shoe part integrally fastened to the wader legs.
Stocking-foot waders are rubber or vinyl pants like panty hose, over
which special wading boots are worn on the feet. Both kinds can provide chest-high protection.

   Each kind has its advocates. Boot-foot waders are bulkier, but
they're usually more durable and less expensive. Stocking-foot waders
are more flexible, and the special boots provide better foot support.
Unfortunately, they're also more easily torn on branches, brambles
and barbed-wire fences. Both can feel like a portable sauna on a hot
day, and a long hike to the river can be a character-building experience.

   Hip boots are adequate for many small streams. They're less expensive and definitely cooler. If you can afford only one pair of
boots, though, get chest waders. They'll give you more freedom in
all sizes and depths of water. And, they build character.

Most boots and waders have cleated rubber soles. These are fine on gravel but dangerous on slippery, bedrock streambeds. The latter are most abundant from the North Fork River on west.

If you'll be wading any water where the streambed is smooth and slippery, be sure to have felts on your soles. Felt-soled boots and waders can be purchased, but they're somewhat expensive. A cheaper alternative is to buy a felt kit and do it yourself. Another option is to attach indoor-outdoor carpet to your soles with Barge cement.

If you do your own felting, first get the cleats ground off at the local tire shop. You may have to wait until the shop fellas stop laughing, but you'll get better adhesion between the felts and soles thatway.

One word of caution about felt- or carpet-soled waders—they're slippery as grease when walking on mud or snow. That's seldom a problem in the Ozarks, but you're bound to bust your derriere sooner or later if you forget.

LANDING NETS

UNLESS you plan to fish without a hook, a landing net is a good idea. You can pay anything from a few dollars to a king's ransom for one.

Any net that's large enough will land a fish, so look for how convenient they are to carry and use. Some have an elastic cord that loops onto your belt or onto a ring on the back of your vest. Others have a clip on the end of the cord. You can hang them at your side, where they're always in the way, or from the back of your neck where they're a little less bothersome. Attaching them to a spring-loaded cord retractor helps.

The main drawback to most nets is that the mesh snags in the brush as you stalk along the bank. You've not been seasoned in the fly-fishing craft until yours catches on a branch, then tears loose and drills you squarely in the middle of the back.

I prefer a folding net that fits in a small holster on a wading belt. It's always out of the way and can't snag on anything. Drawn from the holster, it springs open automatically for instant use. They're reasonably priced and well worth it.

Nets come with either cotton or nylon mesh. Cotton rots from moisture and fish mucus. Nylon doesn't.

Although I favor utility, some folks prefer beauty. Exquisitely crafted nets of laminated walnut, curly maple and other fine woods can be purchased from their creators or commercial outlets. Expect to pay handsomely for the best of them.

If only someone could devise a folding wooden net that could fit in a holster...

FISHING VESTS

WHETHER you'll want a fishing vest depends on how much gear you plan to carry. You don't have to own one just because it's part of the official fly-fishing uniform. Most folks find them handy, though, and there's a wide variety to choose from.

Unless you're willing to buy a new vest fairly often, shop for quality above all else. The fabric should be lightweight and tightly woven. A cotton-and-polyester mix probably is best. Double stitching, especially at stress points like pocket corners, is one of the best signs of quality and durability.

There should be a variety of pocket sizes in easy-to-reach places. Velcro or zippers are preferable to metal snaps. Zippers should have large tabs.

Try the vest for size as if all the pockets were full. You may want to buy a size larger than your normal shirt or coat. Select a style that won't ride up and chafe the back of your neck. For deep wading, a shorty style is better than waist- length. It allows you to get all your pockets wet in deeper water. Ha!

MISCELLANEOUS

FROM THE SOLES of their feet to the peaks of their hats, fly fishers lug a veritable panoply of miscellaneous gear to and from the water. From old gum wrappers to sun-melted lipstick, each item is indispensable to the person who has it.

It's not for me to judge what's necessary for you. A lot of people find the following items useful. The final decision is yours.

Leader Straightener

Leaders and tippets coil when left on the reel for a while. To straighten them out when you arrive at streamside, draw them rapidly through a doubled-over piece of innertube rubber. The frictional heat straightens the coils, allegedly without weakening the materials.

Clippers

You'll want these for trimming line, leader, tippet, oversized flies and jagged fingernails. Buy 'em at the drugstore or get some spring-loaded, clip-on types at your favorite tackle shop.

Hook Hone

Commercially purchased hooks and flies often are disgustingly dull. Even the sharpest can get that way after they've snagged on a rock or two. If you want to hook a high percentage of your strikes, you'll need one of these.

Lead

Even heavily weighted flies may not sink enough in very swift currents. To really work the streambottom effectively, you'll often need some split shot or lead wrap-around on your leader. Casting this extra weight may not be a pretty sight, but sometimes it's the only thing that works.

Although not yet illegal in most places, real lead is gradually losing favor because it's a toxic substance. Substitutes only slightly less heavy are increasingly available.

Dry Fly Floatant

This stuff helps keep your dry flies from getting waterlogged and sinking. It comes as a paste, liquid or aerosol. Don't be without it at hatch time.

Fly Boxes

Use an old tobacco can or baby-food jar if you wish, but nothing beats a specially constructed fly box for keeping your flies orderly and uncrushed.

You have a wide range in style and price to choose from. Most are made to fit in your fishing-vest pockets. Some can be clipped to a belt loop or the outside of your vest.

A few folks prefer a chest fly box. Held on to your chest by straps that criss-cross behind your back, it folds out into a miniature tabletop with several small drawers. Simpler boxes of the same concept can be worn on your belt.

Emergency Wader Patch Kit

Feeling the icy rush of water into your waders is always a special thrill, especially when it's winter and you're miles from the car. Different kinds of wader material require different patching materials. A piece of duct tape or electrical tape often will get you by till you're done for the day.

Surgical Forceps

These are great for extracting deeply lodged hooks—from fish and from yourself.

Polarized Glasses

On some streams, it seems like the sun's always in your eyes, no matter which direction you face. These will help. Equip them with croakies so they don't fall off and swim away.

Hat

Along with polarized glasses, a broad-brimmed or long-billed hat also will help conquer the sun. It'll help fend off heat stroke in the summer and hypothermia in the winter, too. And you'll really appreciate it when a gust of wind tries to drive a big weighted streamer into the back of your head.

Fingerless Gloves

These are indispensable in the winter. Make your own or buy some. Wool is best. It insulates even when wet. For even more winter hand warmth, wear skin-tight latex surgical gloves under them. They're dirt cheap at any drugstore, and keep your hands dry without being clumsy when tying knots.

Rain Gear

Waders are great for keeping the stream out of your socks, but they collect rain like a cistern. A lightweight slicker keeps you dry from head to toe.

Day Packs and Fanny Packs

Some folks shun fishing vests and carry everything in one of these, instead. It's best to get one with pockets on the outside for small, oft-needed items like tippets and flies. That way, you won't be digging your way to the bottom of the main compartment every time you need something.

Soft Luggage

I keep my "sometimes" gear like rain slickers, extra socks and folding wading staffs in a small piece of soft luggage. It's always in the car, so it's never left behind (except when I leave it in the car, but that, too, is character-building). Sure beats trying to remember each item individually when I leave the house.

Wading Staff

Many folks appreciate one of these to lean on when the current's swift or the footing's slippery. Get the sectional, folding kind that's out of the way when you don't need it.

Stream Thermometer

Water temperature has a profound effect on trout behavior and your angling success. A small thermometer in a protective case can help you fit your tactics to the trout's mood of the moment.

Creels, Stringers and Baskets

If you intend to decorate the supper table with trout, you'll need to get them from the water to the car. A wicker creel is the classic way, of course, but they're expensive. Canvas and nylon creels are less elegant, but they're quite functional and reasonably priced.
Nylon and metal stringers are used more commonly. They're a constant aggravation if you move around much, because the fish and current are always wrapping them around your legs. Collapsible wire-mesh baskets are even worse.

THE FLY FISHER'S LIBRARY

YOU CAN TAKE fly and trout fishing as casually or as seriously as you choose. If you aspire to a high level of skill and success, however, one of your most important pieces of equipment will be a library.

I'm not talking about a ragtag stack of newsstand outdoor magazines. I mean a collection of serious books and periodicals on fly-fishing theory, equipment, entomology and tactics, and on trout habitat, life history, behavior and conservation.

There are far more books and magazines than most, if any, of us possibly can afford. Some are written by real masters, but many are not. Most are entertaining, fewer are genuinely instructional, and a rare few are laboriously dull or even marginally literate. Your task is to separate the meat from the bones and scales.

In the way of magazines, here are some suggestions to get you started. There are others, but these are among the best. Subscribe to at least one of them, for sure.

Fly Fisherman

This is the standard against which all other fly-fishing magazines are compared. It covers the entire range of the sport.

Fly Rod & Reel

Another good and pleasantly offbeat magazine that covers the entire range of fly fishing.

American Angler

One of my favorites, if for no other reason than because they've bought more of my articles than any of the others (so you know it's got to be good, right?).

Flyfishing & Tying Journal

A very popular magazine with lots of good information.

Warmwater Fly Fishing

From bass and pike to carp and gar, and everything in between. Trout aren't the only things with fins, and you may enjoy this one, too.

The Flyfisher

This is the Federation of Fly Fishers' magazine, for members only.

Trout

Trout Unlimited publishes this outstanding magazine. It covers the entire range of angling for all coldwater species, with major emphasis on conservation.

In previous editions, I risked recommending some of the better books available. Recent years, however, have witnessed a veritable flood of new titles, and the trend seems likely to continue. My best advice is to ask other knowledgeable fly fishers for their recommendations, or try to borrow theirs (except for this tome, of course, which will delight us both if you buy a copy).

In addition to books and magazines, you also may want to add instructional videocassettes to your library. Watching fly-fishing experts and their gear in motion can tell you a lot that inanimate words, illustrations and photographs can't.

As with books, there are too many good (and poor) videos to mention, and new ones are coming on the market constantly. Again, try to borrow as many as you can. Some fly shops will rent them to you, instead of only selling them.

And that's as far as I'm willing to go in the way of specific recommendations. Good luck!

GEAR AND TACKLE CARE

GEAR AND TACKLE care are essential to your trout-stalking pleasure and success.

Fly Rod Care

Your rod requires more care than any other piece of equipment. Fortunately, it's more common sense than time-consuming hard work.

Two of the most vicious fly-rod predators are carelessly slammed car doors and trunk lids. The surest defense against them is a rod case. The best are made of tube aluminum with a screw cap. Plastic ones can be purchased less expensively, but some of them may warp if left in a sealed car on a hot day. You can economically build your own from a section of stout PVC pipe with screw caps. Always put your rod in a heavy cloth sleeve before casing it.

Few things are more invisible than a rod lying on the ground. Even if you know where it is, other people don't. Lean it against a tree, log or rock, or hang it securely over some limbs where it won't get stepped on. It's just common sense, but lots of folks forget.

The most fragile part of your rod is the tip. Treat it gently. Steady pressure and flexing won't harm it, but a sharp rap may. If you hang your fly on the far shore, try to retrieve it with a steady tug instead of whiplike jerks. Better yet, point the rod straight at the fly and pull on the line directly. It's cheaper to break off a fly than a rod tip.

Check the guide wraps regularly for signs of wear. If they're frayed or if a guide seems loose, head straight for a shop that offers quality rodbuilding and repair service.

Be sure the ferrules connecting the rod sections fit snugly. Few things are more embarrassing than watching your rod's tip section follow the fly across the water. Push the fittings straight together and pull them straight apart. Twisting scrapes away the fitting parts until they're no longer snug. Keep the ferrules free of abrasive grit, too.

You also may want to refinish your rod every now and then. It's mostly for cosmetic effect, but the finish does provide some protection against sharp objects. The drawback to brightly finished rods is that they can flash in the sun while casting, sometimes spooking the fish.

With reasonable caution and a little tender, loving care, your fly rod can last a lifetime. It sure is less expensive that way.

Reel Care

Sand and grit are your reel's worst enemies. When not in your hand, suspend your rod and reel over a log or branch if you can. If you must lay your reel on the ground, put it on a clean rock or inside your hat instead of in the gravel.

Periodically take the reel apart and clean it, even though there's no outward sign of trouble. Lubricate the moving parts with a light grease. Do not use oil, which could spread onto your line.

Many reels have screw-in spool posts which can loosen and fall out. There's nothing worse when a fish is on. Use Wick N' Lock (made by Loctite) or a similar product to hold the post securely. Similarly, some reel bases are attached to the rest of the reel with screws rather than rivets. Use the same solution for the same problem.

When not in use, reels are best stored in a zippered case or cloth bag with a drawstring. Keep them in your vest so they're never forgotten when you leave home.

Wader Care

Waders have several enemies besides brambles and barbed-wire fences. Heat and prolonged moisture on the inside are two. Store your waders in a cool place, hanging upside-down so air can circulate in them.

If you really give them a dunking, try stuffing towels or newspapers tightly into the feet to soak up the worst of the moisture first. Blowing air into them by reversing a tank-type vacuum cleaner is better if one's handy. Blow-driers sometimes help in a pinch, but don't let too much heat build up. Above all, don't put the drier down in the waders where it sits in its own heat. You'll likely be in the market for a new one if you do.

Ozone is the unseen enemy that destroys rubber. Dry waders can be kept in a tightly sealed plastic trash bag or in a commercially available wader-storage pouch.

Tire patches are best for fixing leaks in all-rubber waders, but they're not much good on vinyl-coated ones. One of the best products for patching vinyl is called Shoe Patch (made by Kiwi). Find it at tackle stores, shoe-repair shops and discount stores.

Wader legs longer than your own often rub through between your thighs and knees. You can reinforce these spots with tire patches or pieces of nylon stocking embedded in Shoe Patch.

Fly Line Care

Heat, abrasion and solvents are the destructive forces here. Never leave your line in a closed-up car in the hot sun. The heat will melt and crack your line just as surely as it will the candy bar you also left in there.

The next precaution is to walk on your line as little as possible. Sounds obvious, but we all do it sooner or later, even though we know better. We get so intent on fishing that we lose track of all the line lying on the gravel in front of us. Don't scrape or wrap it tightly around rocks, logs, branches or broken beer bottles, either.

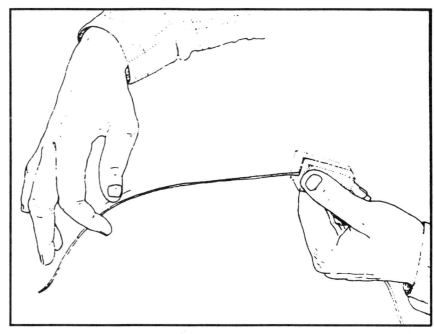

Clean your floating line regularly.

The solvents in some dry-fly floatants and insect repellants can damage your line, too. Be careful which way you spray them, and clean your hands thoroughly after their use.

With use, dirt and algae build up on floating lines, causing them to sink. Clean them periodically according to manufacturer's instructions. Not all lines should be cleaned the same way.

Leaders and Tippet Material

Leaders and tippet material weaken with age. Throw yours away once or twice a year, especially if they've been exposed to the sun for long periods. Replace them with new material that you're fairly sure hasn't been out of the factory too long.

Landing Net Care

The main problem with landing nets is that the mesh tears and rots. Only caution can prevent the first. For the second, always wash the fish mucus off at the end of the day, and then let the mesh dry before or during storage. Replacement mesh is commercially available, so you don't have to throw the entire net away if the mesh goes bad.

Fly Boxes

Fly boxes have a variety of different clasps, some of which are more durable than others. I've not seen any yet that are easily repaired. A rubber band is a terrible substitute. You'd best get a new box.

Clipper Care

Sooner or later, you'll probably use your clippers for something you really shouldn't. When you do, you'll put a pretty big nick in the cutting edges. If you must, put it in the end of the edges rather than the middle. That way, the edges can still operate pretty much like they're supposed to without a lot of fumbling around. To look at some folks' clippers, you'd think they use them to keep score of their fish like the Old West gunfighters kept score of their victims.

THE TROUT'S AQUATIC CUISINE

MANY FOLKS THINK TROUT live out their lives on a diet of corn, garlic cheese and party marshmallows. For the first week or two out of the hatchery, bits of gravel the size and color of pellet food are a common favorite. A former state-record rainbow was taken on a french fry and a piece of lye soap. Are these what trout really eat?

There's no denying that these bizarre items are among the last things that many trout eat, but what do they live on the rest of the time? Fortunately, Missouri's streams abound in more common but equally tasty culinary delights.

Aquatic insects are a major portion of the trout's diet, especially during the early years. With increasing age and size, larger morsels such as minnows and crayfish become more important, but insects are never totally abandoned.

All aquatic insects go through a series of different life stages from egg to adult. Most species have an annual life cycle, but some have several generations per year, and a few take up to two years to complete the process.

Four general types of aquatic insects stand above all others in their angling importance. The most legendary is the mayfly, of which Missouri has 92 different species. The immature nymphs spend their lives among the rocks on the bottom, then rise to the surface to produce the classic hatches about which dry-fly fishers have waxed poetic for centuries.

Just as important in most Missouri streams are caddisflies. The immature larvae and pupae of some species encase themselves in miniature homes of sticks, sand or gravel on the streambottom, while other kinds spin fine

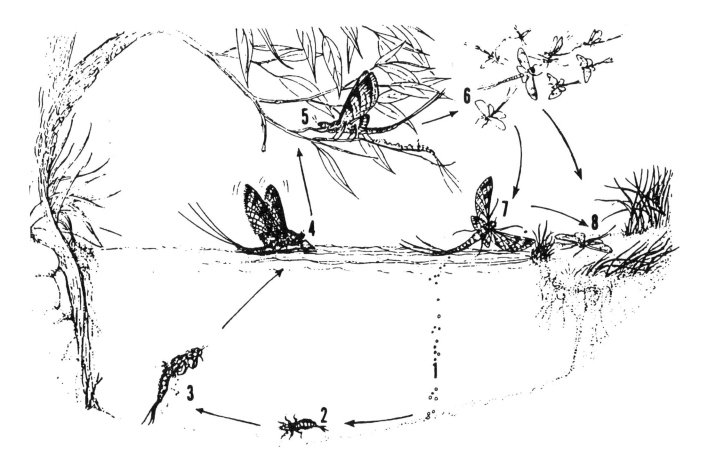

MAYFLY LIFE CYCLE: Life begins as an egg which settles to the streambottom (1). In about two weeks, the eggs hatch into nymphs (2) which live among the rocks and debris on the bottom. The nymphs moult (shed their skins) many times as they grow and mature.

After a year for most species (more or less, for a few), the nymphs leave the bottom and ascend to the surface to emerge (3). Most species ascend directly up through the water, but a few crawl out onto a rock, stick or the shore. In the process, they shed their nymphal skins and become winged duns (4), more technically called subimagos.

As soon as the dun's wings are extended and dry enough for flight, most species fly to shoreline vegetation and moult a final time (5) into fully mature spinners or imagos. A few species moult in flight rather than at rest.

The spinners then swarm over the water and mate in flight (6) after which the females lay their eggs either above, on or under the water surface, depending on species (7). Both sexes then die, usually within twenty-four to forty-eight hours of emergence (8).

silken webs to trap food like a spider. The adults look like tiny moths.

Stoneflies are less numerous than the others, but several species are important because of their large size. The nymph of one, the giant black stonefly, grows to a length of almost two inches before transforming into the airborne adult.

—44—

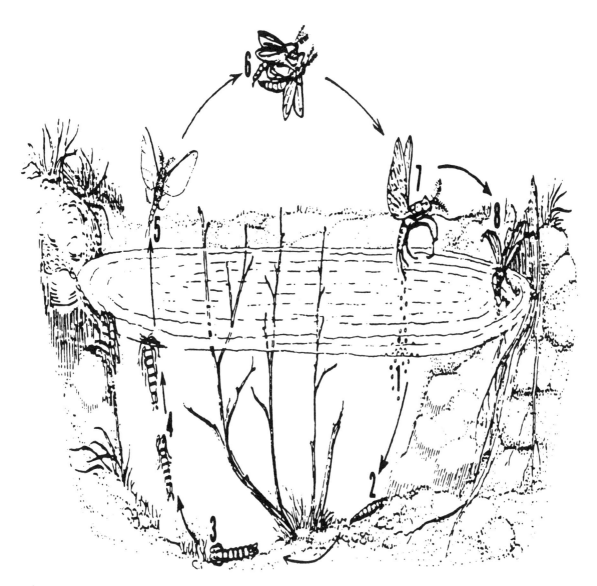

CADDISFLY LIFE CYCLE: Life begins as an egg which either settles to, or is laid directly on, the streambottom, depending on species (1). The eggs quickly hatch into larvae (2) which build protective cases of sand, gravel or bits of vegetation on or in the bottom (3).

After a year for most species (less than that for a few), the larvae retreat within their cases and pupate for a couple of weeks. When the change is completed, the pupae leave their cases and ascend to the surface (4), shedding their pupal skins in the process.

The fully mature adults fly to shoreline vegetation (5) and mate sporadically during the next couple of weeks (6). The females then lay their eggs above, on or beneath the water surface, depending on species (7). Both sexes then die (8).

Dipterans are also important aquatic insects. Mosquitos, deerflies, blackflies and horseflies are familiar members of this group. Gnats and no-see-ums are typical of the many tiny kinds of dipterans. The largest of this group is the cranefly. Its larva is a long, pudgy, brownish worm that lives in the gravel. The adult resembles an enormous mosquito.

STONEFLY LIFE CYCLE: Life begins as an egg which settles to the stream-bottom (1). The eggs quickly hatch into nymphs (2) which live among the rocks and debris on the bottom, moulting many times as they grow and develop.

After one to two years, depending on species, the nymphs crawl up on a rock or the shore (3) and moult into winged adults (4). Mating occurs on streamside vegetation or in flight (5). The females lay their eggs above or on the water surface (6), after which both sexes die (7).

Helgrammites are seldom abundant but, like stoneflies, are important because of their large size. They're the larval form of the dobsonfly. Dragonfly and damselfly nymphs are other examples of occasional, but large, aquatic insects.

To learn the most common forms of aquatic insect life in your favorite streams, pick big stones out of the riffles and look on the undersides. Better yet, make yourself a small net of fine-mesh screenwire on a stout frame, or buy one from a fly fishing-supply mail-order house. Hold it firmly against the bottom in a riffle, then stir up the gravel and cobbles upstream from it with your feet or a three-pronged garden rake. The critters in and on the bottom will be swept into the net where you can pick them out for study.

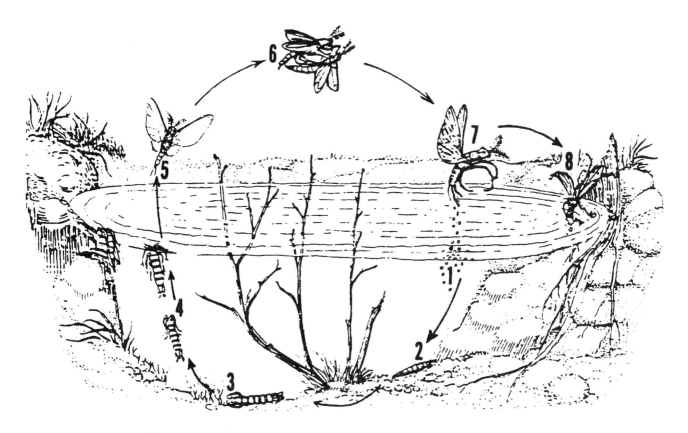

DIPTERAN LIFE CYCLE: Life begins as an egg which settles to the streambottom (1). The eggs soon hatch into larvae (2) which live among the
rocks and debris on the bottom.
   In a year or less, depending on species, the larvae pupate for a brief
period (3), then emerge (4) as winged adults (5). Mating usually occurs
in flight (6), after which the females lay their eggs (7) and both sexes
die (8).

Do the same thing around heavy watercress and weed beds.
   Insects aren't all you'll find in your net. Crustaceans like freshwater shrimp (scuds) may also show up there, especially if you've been
stirring around in watercress beds.
   Crayfish, of course, are likely to show up almost anywhere. Cressbugs, which also are crustaceans rather than bugs, are common weedbed
inhabitants. Snails, too, are an important part of many trouts' diet.
   Many folks are surprised to learn there's an aquatic counterpart to
that old angling standby, the earthworm. It's called an oligochaete,
and it looks pretty much like its land-bound cousin.
   Many kinds of small fish inhabit Missouri's trout streams. The ones
you'll most commonly find in your sampling net are various species of
sculpins and darters. Minnows and shiners are common, too, but they
usually inhabit slower waters than you'll be sampling. All of these
small fish, including young of their own kind, are favorite trout prey.
   Don't ignore terrestrial insects in your study of natural trout
foods. They're extremely important, especially during summer and fall.

Grasshoppers come in different sizes and colors. Along with katydids and crickets, they often blunder into the water. Ants are perennial favorites. Cicadas are avidly eaten during the years they hatch in abundance. Japanese beetles and box elder bugs also abound in some years and eventually find their way into the trout's feeding territories. In fact, there are few living things of small size that trout won't eat if given the opportunity.

The best time of year for studying aquatic life is from late fall through early spring. Many kinds of insects emerge from mid-April through July, so they're hard to find for several months thereafter. They're also more numerous before the spring floods than after, and the individuals are largest just before they hatch. Non-insect critters like freshwater shrimp and cressbugs also wax and wane with time.

The study of aquatic and terrestrial trout foods can be a fascinating pursuit. You don't have to make an all-consuming passion out of it, although some folks do. For beginners, one of the most comprehensive yet understandable references I know is Dave Whitlock's Guide to Aquatic Trout Foods (Nick Lyons Winchester Press, 1982, ISBN 0-87691-377-0.

THE FLY FISHER'S FAKE CUISINE

WHAT'S THE BEST FLY for Missouri trout? Everybody wants to know, but it's a question without an answer.

A so-so fly presented to the trout with excellent technique will be consistently more effective than an excellent fly presented poorly. To compound the problem, what's excellent technique on one day may be poor on another, even with the same fly.

Many other factors besides presentation technique also influence how well a fly pattern produces. What are the main kinds of natural trout food where you're casting? Is the current slow or fast? Is the water clear or cloudy? Are the trout newly stocked or old veterans? Are they little tykes or lunkers? How frightened are they? These are just a few of the questions you'll need to consider when selecting a fly.

Flies can be categorized in a number of different ways, and the differences among categories aren't always clear. Don't be intimidated by the jargon. You'll catch on soon enough.

One way to break them down is into imitations and attractors. Imitations bear some reasonable resemblance to a specific natural trout food, at least in the angler's opinion. Attractors don't. They look like some sort of bug or other natural food in general, but nothing in particular. No one really knows what the trout think about the difference. Maybe the professional pollsters can find out someday, possibly with an exit interview.

Imitations vary in their portrayal of reality. A few fly tiers specialize in crafting imitations which are virtually indistinguishable from the real thing. Most, though, actually are caricatures. The major features are roughly the same size, shape and color of the real thing, but that's where the similarity ends. Fortunately, trout ignore the difference often enough to perpetuate the sport.

Another way to categorize flies is into dry and wet. Dry flies float on the water surface. Wet flies sink. There's also a category which sort of falls in between. It's sometimes called the slightly-wets or almost-dries.

Dry Flies

Some dries imitate mayflies as they ride the water surface, drying their wings for flight. These are called duns. Others imitate dead mayflies after they've mated and fallen back to the surface. These are called spentwings or spinners.

Dry caddisfly patterns imitate either the dead adult or egg-laying female. There's no special name for them other than dry caddis.

Spiders and skaters make up another category of dry flies. They're most commonly thought to imitate adult craneflies, but that's arguable sometimes.

Size 20 or smaller dry flies often are called midges in reference to their small size.

Many dry flies are attractors rather than imitations.

The Royal Wulff,
a famous attractor dry fly

The Light Cahill, a dry fly
which imitates several mayfly species

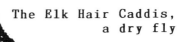

The Elk Hair Caddis,
a dry fly

Wet Flies

Although the definition of wet flies can include anything that sinks, the term usually is restricted to those which, with a few exceptions, have hair or feather wings sweeping over the back. Viewed realistically, they're often more attractor than imitation. Wooly worms, shrimp and cressbugs are examples of unwinged wet flies.

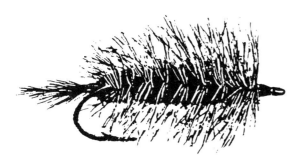

The Leadwing Coachman,
a winged wet fly

The Wooly Worm, an
unwinged attractor wet fly

Nymphs

Nymphs are sinking flies that resemble the early life stages of mayflies, stoneflies, dragonflies and damselflies. Some patterns are fairly imitative, others are more generalized.

The Tellico Nymph, which
resembles many nymphs in
general but none in particular.

The Boulder Roller Nymph, a large
rubber-legged imitation of the
Giant Black Stonefly

Emergers, Floating Nymphs, Stillborns and Pupae

These are the slightly-wets and almost-dries. Emergers imitate the mayfly's life stage as it changes from nymph to dun. During the change, it leaves the streambottom and swims or floats to the surface. The fly is presented in the same manner, or just beneath the surface.

Floating nymphs imitate the mayfly as it reaches the water surface and begins to shed its nymphal shell. Stillborns are a special kind of floating nymph that imitates a drowned mayfly which was only partially successful in escaping from its shell.

Caddisflies emerge like mayflies, but they're called caddis pupae rather than caddis emergers. In the same manner, emerging midges are called midge pupae. In this case, the term midge refers to aquatic insects of the Order Diptera.

Soft Hackle fly,
thought by many to
imitate emerging
caddisflies

March
Brown
Emerger

Streamers and Bucktails

Traditionally, streamers are sinking flies tied with feathers to resemble minnows and other small fish. Bucktails resemble small fish, too, but they're tied with deer or other animal hair instead of feathers.

In recent years, some non-fish imitations have also come to be regarded as streamers. The most common examples are Wooly Buggers and leeches.

The Thunder Creek, a bucktail streamer

Terrestrials

These flies imitate non-aquatic insects such as grasshoppers, ants, beetles, houseflies and inchworms which commonly fall or are blown into the water. Most are tied as dry flies, but a few are tied as wets.

Black ant tied as a wet fly

None of the Above

Although not everyone will agree, I've chosen to describe some flies as none-of-the-above. Mostly, they imitate aquatic critters which are neither insect nor fish. Crayfish and leeches are the most common examples. Shrimp (scuds) and cressbugs (sowbugs) might also be included here rather than in the wet-fly category.

One highly effective dry fly for monster brown trout is a swimming mouse imitation.

Every fly-fisher"s dream, of course, is to encounter a trout big enough to engulf a full-grown muskrat. I'm not sure how to imitate, much less cast, one of these. But I'm working on it.

Freshwater shrimp imitation

Freshwater shrimp, also known as a scud

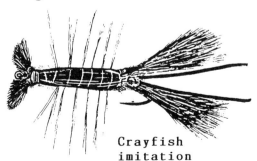

Crayfish imitation

THE MISSOURI ANGLER'S BASIC TROUT-FLY SELECTION

THERE ARE uncounted thousands of different fly patterns, and all of them can be tied in more than one hook size. All will catch a trout sometime, somewhere. The hard truth, though, is that most patterns are designed to catch the angler's fancy as much as the fish's.

Although there are many other excellent flies, the following list should serve you well most of the time. I carry others, too, but these are indispensable.

Dry Flies

       Adams, size 12 and 16
       Red Quill, size 14
       Light Cahill, size 12 and 16
       Renegade, size 14 or 16
       Griffith's Gnat, size 20
       Elk Hair Caddis, size 12 and 16
         (in my opinion, the single
         best all-around Missouri dry fly)

Adams

Wet Flies

       Wooly Bugger, olive, size 8 or 10
         (the single best all-around
         Missouri trout fly)
       BUBfly, size 8 or 10 (use only in
         the commercial fee-fishing areas)
       Scud (freshwater shrimp), olive or
         orange, sizes 12 to 18

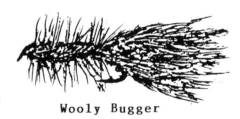

Wooly Bugger

Nymphs

       Prince, size 12 or 14
       Red Squirrel, size 10 and 14
       Gold Ribbed Hare's Ear, size 12
       Any dark weighted stonefly
         pattern, 1 to 1½ inches long

Red Squirrel Nymph

Emergers and Pupae

       Soft Hackle, gold or peacock and
         partridge, size 14
       Copper John, size 12 and 16
       Midge pupa, size 20

Soft hackle

Streamers and Bucktails

       Thunder Creek Silver Shiner, size 8
       Olive Matuka, size 8 or 10
       Zonker, size 8 or 10
       Any sculpin imitation, size 2 to 8

Matuka Streamer

Terrestrials

Black ant

      Grasshopper, yellow, size 8 to 12
      Black Ant, size 14 or 16

None of the Above

      Crayfish, size 4 to 10

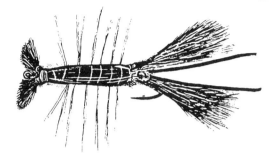

WHAT'S THE HATCH?

MATCH THE HATCH. It's one of trout stalking's most famous admoni-
tions. What's it about?
    Aquatic insect life begins on or in the streambottom as an egg, and
goes through several transformations there. Eventually, the time
comes for the insect to leave the water and take to the air for
mating.
    Insects such as caddisflies, most mayflies and most dipterans swim
or float from the bottom to the surface to fly away. Others such as
stoneflies, craneflies and a few mayflies crawl up on a rock or out on
the bank for flight. In either case, hundreds or thousands of a species all leaving the water together is called an emergence or a hatch
(actually, an emergence creates a hatch). Under favorable circumstances, the air can be literally filled with clouds of emerging insects.
    The classical hatches are those where the insects swim or float from
the bottom to the surface. The insects are easily visible and highly
vulnerable to predators at this time, especially if they have to ride
the surface for some distance before their wings are ready for flight.
Trout often go into a feeding frenzy.
    Hatches of aquatic insects which crawl out of the water for flight
entice the trout in a different way. In this case, they're exposed
and vulnerable while crawling or swimming to shore, and large numbers
of them may fall or be blown back into the water.
    After mating, the adults return to the water as a group to lay eggs
and die. The stream is again awash with insects, and trout gorge
themselves then, too. This is not called a hatch, however. When mayflies do it, it's called a spinner fall. There's no name for it with
other insects.
    In recent years, it's become semi-chic to refer to terrestrial-
insect hatches, too. You may hear or read of the "grasshopper hatch"
or "flying-ant hatch." All this describes is a sudden abundance of
these important trout foods on or near the water.
    On any given stream, different species of aquatic insects emerge at
fairly predictable times of the year and hours of the day. The
hatches often continue for several weeks or months.

MISSOURI TROUT-STREAM HATCHES

THE FLY-FISHING IMPORTANCE of a particular insect's emergence or hatch depends upon several factors. Some very small insects are important because they emerge in great concentrations, enticing the trout by their abundance. Less-abundant insects may be important if they're individually large enough to be a sizeable mouthful.

Insects that swim or float from the streambottom to the surface generally are more available to trout than those that crawl up on a rock or the bank for flight. Those that characteristically exit the water slowly and awkwardly rather than swiftly are more vulnerable and thus more important. And for most fly fishers, insects that emerge during the daylight hours are more important than those that emerge at night.

My first two editions of this epistle dwelt in great detail on Missouri's trout-stream insects and their hatching characteristics. If you enjoyed that, or thought it was I-can't-live-another-day-without-it information, you may be sorely disappointed by what comes next in this edition. Stay with me, now. I'm gonna tell you like it really is, not like all the other writers would have you believe it is.

Most of us are indoctrinated to believe that hatch matching is a contest between us and the fish. If we're highly skilled in our fly-fishing craft, we win—always. Any skill level short of the book and magazine writers' self-proclaimed prowess, however, and the fish win. We're supposed to slink away with our tails tucked between our legs, stunned by befuddlement at the best, burdened by eternally shattered self esteem at the worst. Buh-lo-nee!

Truth is, hatch matching is more of a game we play with ourselves than with the fish, too often carrying it to extremes far beyond what the fish care about. Now, then—if that gives you pleasure, don't let me talk you out of it. Happiness in any form is to be treasured. If you're of a more practical bent, however, there's just as much happiness to be found in what comes next.

Mayflies

Mayflies have fascinated fly fishers for centuries, and many kinds have acquired common names in addition to their scientific ones. Some names describe the dun's appearance (blue-winged olive), some names honor the originator of the dun imitation (Quill Gordon, for Theodore Gordon) or someone else (Hendrickson, for A.E. Hendrickson). Others are somewhat whimsical (white-gloved howdy). The largest mayflies are sometimes called drakes. The names apply to the feathered imitations as well.

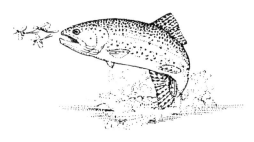

As of this writing, Missouri's official mayfly list counted more than ninety species. Over half occur in Ozark trout country. Over fifty are newly discovered since my second edition. Even many of the previously known ones have new scientific names now, and many have multiple common names. The only people who can tell most of them

apart are professional entomologists armed with high-powered micro-
scopes. Sorry—even the other writers' oft-cited "highly educated"
trout don't fall into that category.
   So, let's get real. Here are the only mayfly hatches you're likely
to be interested in matching here in Missouri, explained by their common fly-fishing names.

Hendrickson

   The Hendricksons (Ephemerella subvaria) are an eagerly anticipated,
early-season, afternoon hatch. They begin sporadically as early as
late February, more commonly in late March or April, peak in late
April or early May, and sometimes continue into early June. The Light
Hendrickson pattern imitates the female dun, the Red Quill pattern
imitates the male dun. Carry both in sizes 12-14.

Blue-winged Olive

   The Blue-winged Olives (primarily Baetis spp., but some other stuff,
too) probably hatch for more of the year than any of the other mayflies. They commonly begin in March, peak in June and July, and carry
on into November. I still remember, however, watching them pop up between my knees in a driving, mid-January sleet storm at Montauk State
Park many years ago. Mid-day into evening is their favorite time of
day. Carry the imitations in sizes 14-18.

Light Cahill

   At least half a dozen species (Stenonema and Stenacron spp.) are
effectively imitated by the traditional Light Cahill pattern in sizes
12-16. The hatches sometimes begin in late April, more commonly in
May, peak in June and July, and continue into late fall. Some species
hatch all day long, others in the afternoon or evening.

Tiny White-winged Black

   Also known as Tricos (Tricorythodes sp.),
these diminutive (size 24) mayflies hatch
around dawn or before from May into fall,
and you may encounter up-your-nose-and-in-
your-ears mating-flight clouds of them
dancing over the water on very-early summer mornings. Some folks report doing well
with spentwing imitations, but you sure
couldn't prove it by me.

Mayfly dun

Pale Evening Dun or Sulfur

These are yellowish mayflies of two different species. Ephemerella invaria leads off the hatch on May and June afternoons. Match it in sizes 12-14. As invaria wanes, the smaller Ephemerella dorothea comes on in the evening during June and July. Match it in size 16.

Leadwing Coachman, Slate Drake and White-gloved Howdy

These (Isonychia spp.) are some of our larger (sizes 10-12), and most common, trout-stream mayflies. Mid-day to evening hatching begins in June, peaks in July, and continues into October.

White Fly

Fishing the White Fly (Ephoron spp.) hatch is a real kick when you can find it. Sometimes beginning in late August, more often in early September, and extending into mid-October, imitate it with an all-white mayfly pattern in sizes 12-14. You don't have to get up early for this one—late afternoon into early evening is when it happens.

Caddisflies

Missouri's trout-stream caddisfly species number well over half a hundred, ranging from the huge (sizes 4-6) Great Dive Bomber Sedge (Agrypnia sp.) down to the tiny (size 24-26) microcaddis (Hydroptila spp.). At least one kind or another hatches every month of the year. Almost all of them hatch during July. What's a hatch matcher to do?

Dry caddisfly patterns are tied in many different styles—clipped-hair, hair-wing, delta-wing, down-wing, tent-wing and so on. By a wide margin, the most popular among Missouri fly fishers is the Elk Hair Caddis, a hair-wing pattern that can be adapted to imitate most of our important caddisfly species.

Our single most abundant trout-stream caddisfly is the Little Sister Sedge (Cheumatopsyche spp.). It hatches in the afternoon from March into December, peaking from June through September. Regardless of what tying style you choose, imitate it with brown wings and legs, and a green body, in sizes 14-16.

We have one all-white caddisfly known as the White Miller (Nectopsyche spp.). It hatches at night from May into November, peaking in July and August. Fish the all-white imitation in sizes 12-14.

Things get real simple from here on out. Virtually all of our remaining caddisflies of any significance have brown wings, and most have brown legs, too. Carry a lot of imitations with brown bodies and a few with yellow bodies, all in sizes 12-16, and you'll be pretty well prepared to match any worthwhile caddisfly hatch you're likely to encounter.

Stoneflies

Although Missouri's trout streams harbor at least sixteen species of stoneflies ranging from size-2 to size-24, the only one I know of that hatches very often in fishable concentrations is the Little Yellow Stonefly (Isoperla dicala). Fish a clear-winged, yellow-bodied and tan-legged imitation in sizes 16-18 during April, May and June to match it.

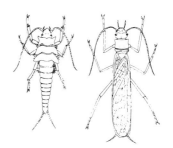

Stonefly
nymph and adult

Dipterans

Dipterans—midges—come in myriad descriptions and emerge in one form or another year 'round. Within reason, almost anything tied on a size 20 or smaller hook will pass as some sort of midge imitation. The Griffith's Gnat is a favorite pattern with many.

Craneflies (Tipula spp.) are the exception to the rule for dipterans. They emerge from late April through June. The imitations of choice are Spiders, Skaters or Dave's Adult Cranefly. Regardless of what size hook they're tied on, a hackle diameter of 1 to 1½ inches is appropriate.

USING THE HATCH INFORMATION

IF YOU'RE NEW to the gambit of matching the hatch, here are some pointers on how to use the emergence information.

The emergence, or hatch, information applies to the trout-holding portion of the Missouri Ozarks in general. Many of the species are more abundant in some streams than in others. Even the same species can emerge at different times in different nearby streams or at different places in the same stream. Hatches near the Arkansas border may precede the same hatches farther north by a week, sometimes two. Hatches of all kinds are more prolific in years without high water than in years when floods churn and scour the streambed.

Some folks mistakenly believe that the emergence information tells what time of the year certain fly patterns should be fished. In reality, it only tells approximately when to have various fly patterns in your vest in case you chance upon major hatch and fish-feeding activity. If there's no hatch on, or if nothing's feeding on a hatch, you don't have to fish an imitation just because it's recommended. Missouri's trout are seldom very selective in their feeding preferences, in spite of what many writers would have you believe.

The traditional perception is that hatch time is dry-fly time. That's when dry-fly fishers usually do their best, but it's not true that they always do better than everyone else. Actually, the emerger, pupa, floating nymph and stillborn fly patterns will often outproduce the traditional dry patterns at this time.

I admit to the special beauty and pleasure in fishing the traditional dry fly. I encourage you, however, to give these other patterns a fair try. Skillfully fished, they also add a special charm and excitement to the fly-fishing sport.

MATCH THE MINNOWS, TOO

MISSOURI'S TROUT STREAMS abound in minnows, and they're a favorite on the trouts' menu. At least thirty-five species are common; several others are present in lesser numbers.

Biologists classify these small fish into four main groups. The Family Cyprinidae—the true minnows—is represented by nineteen common species. The Family Cyprinodontidae—the killifishes—has two common representatives. The Family Cottidae is represented by two species of sculpins. The Family Percidae includes twelve common species of darters.

Many of these thirty-five species are similar in size, appearance and behavior, so they can be lumped into just a few groups for the fly fisher's deceptive purposes.

Both sexes of nineteen species, and the females of nearly all, maintain the same appearance year 'round. In the other sixteen species, males take on brilliant shades of red and orange during the spawning season, and fly fishers who imitate their distinctive appearance often do well, especially on big trout. The period from mid-April to mid-June is when you'll find most of these in their spawning colors.

For fly-imitation purposes, I've lumped these important fish into five groups. I hope you'll have as much fun with them as I have.

The Dark-backed Silvery Minnows

This group is characterized by dark-olive, olive-brown or black backs, silvery sides with or without a prominent midline, white bellies, plain fins and a slender silhouette. Adults reach an average length of about three inches. They're well imitated by Zonker and Thunder Creek patterns tied with these features. The following species make up this group:

creek chub   telescope shiner
southern redbelly dace   wedgespot shiner
rosyface shiner

The Light-backed Silvery Minnows

This group has backs of greenish-yellow, olive-yellow, olive, light olive-brown or tan. Adults grow to about four inches. Otherwise, its members are identical to the dark-backed silvery minnows. Again, Zonker and Thunder Creek patterns tied with the distinctive colors are excellent imitations. This group includes these species:

bigeye chub   whitetail shiner
streamline chub   Ozark shiner
bleeding shiner   Ozark minnow
duskystripe shiner   bluntnose minnow
striped shiner   central stoneroller
redfin shiner   largescale stoneroller
bigeye shiner   northern studfish
steelcolor shiner   blackspotted topminnow

Sculpins

The only thing in the world that looks like a sculpin is another sculpin. Missouri's are vertically banded or mottled in shades of tan, reddish-brown, olive-brown and dark brown. The bellies are off-white, and the lower fins are tan. Their shape is similar to a catfish's, with a large head and large pectoral fins. Adults grow to four inches, occasionally longer. The Muddler Minnow and Whitlock's Sculpin are the imitations of choice. Missouri's species are the mottled and banded sculpins.

Darters

Darters are interesting little fish that often appear to walk along the streambottom on their large pectoral fins. Missouri's species are diverse in their coloration, but the banded or mottled sculpin patterns tied in a slender, minnowlike shape would resemble many of them. The maximum adult length varies from three to four inches. The group includes the following species:

slenderhead darter
greenside darter
stippled darter
Missouri saddled darter
Arkansas saddled darter
orangethroat darter

logperch
yoke darter
gilt darter
rainbow darter
banded darter
fantail darter

The Brilliant Spawning Males

These beautiful fish are characterized by generally dark backs and sides, bellies and lower fins of red, reddish-orange or orange. Some have a prominent dark midline; others don't. Adult size goes up to about four inches. The most common imitations are Red Matuka, Dark Spruce, Baby Brook Trout and Baby Rainbow streamers, but bucktails and other common patterns can be adapted to the appropriate color schemes. This group includes the following species:

largescale stoneroller
central stoneroller
southern redbelly dace
duskystripe shiner
Missouri saddled darter
Arkansas saddled darter
orangethroat darter
stippled darter

creekchub
rosyface shiner
bleeding shiner
striped shiner
Ozark minnow
gilt darter
yoke darter
rainbow darter

For more details on these fishes' descriptions, spawning habits, other life history and favored habitats, get a copy of Bill Pflieger's The Fishes of Missouri (Missouri Department of Conservation, 1997, ISBN 1-887247-11-4). You'll find it an endless source of fascination and a valuable trout-fishing reference.

The Whitlock Sculpin,
an imitative streamer

The Zonker

BARBLESS HOOKS—SHOULD I?

ONE OF THE BIGGEST MYTHS in angling is that the fish will get off if there's no barb on the hook. Nonsense. The reasons for using barbless hooks are several, and they're all good.

The first step in catching a trout is to get the hook into it. You're going to hook most of them somewhere in the lip where the flesh is tough and bony. A slender hook penetrates more easily than a fat one. Liken the barbless hook to a slender finishing nail and the barbed one to a spike. Which is easier to drive into a board?

But won't a barbless hook pull out? There's no reason why it should. Just think of how big a twist it takes to back a hook out the way it went in. As long as there's any kind of line tension between you and the fish, there's no way the hook can twist enough to back its way out. The only reason you'll ever lose a fish on a barbless hook is that it tore out. That's going to happen just as often with a barbed one— maybe more often because of the poorer penetration.

Even the expert anglers you read about or see on TV catch a lot more small and average-size fish than big ones. They just don't tell you about them. Wherever there's a legal-length limit, you're going to release more fish than you keep, just because there are always more of the sub-legal ones.

Like the mighty oak and the acorn, big trout can only grow from small ones. That being the case, there's no sense in tearing up the little ones any more than necessary. Barbless hooks can be extracted more easily, without a lot of damage and rough handling, often without even touching the fish. That means more and bigger trout for all of us.

Many fly fishers are catching onto the advantages of barbless hooks. Only a few shops carry barbless flies in stock, but several of the big mail-order places do. If you tie your own, or have a friend who ties for you, they're easily available. Otherwise, just crimp the barb down with needlenose pliers.

If you're still not sure, try an experiment. Visit a fee-fishing area or bluegill pond where you can always catch another if the first one gets off. Try both kinds of hooks and keep score. If you're not convinced by the end of the day, then stay with what you've got.

SHOULD I TIE MY OWN?

THOUSANDS of folks do.
It's a business for some.
For most, it's lots of
fun, satisfaction and
economy.

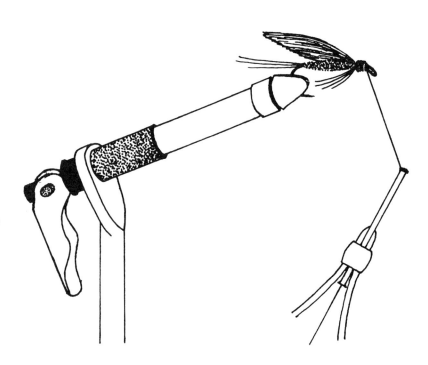

Don't get uptight a-
bout having no talent,
poor eyesight or ten
thumbs. Most trout
aren't nearly as finicky
about a fly's appearance
as fly casters are.
There are ways for most
people to get around the
problem of poor eyesight,
and some of the best-
known tiers in American
fly-fishing history had
hands that looked like
grappling hooks. Even
if you use the highest-
quality, most expensive
materials, you still
can save up to eighty
percent or more on your
fly costs.

Chances are, someone near you will be glad to help you get started.
Ask around. I've never met a tier yet who wasn't flattered to pass the
craft on to someone else. Most fly shops are heavily stocked with
many excellent fly-tying books and videos.

FLY CARE

FLIES CAN BE a major expense, so you'll want to make them last as long
as possible.

Check the hook points constantly. If you're repeatedly missing
strikes, maybe the point is dull, rusty, bent or even missing. A hone
can help solve the first two problems, and a strong fingernail or forceps may solve the third. There's no known cure for the last, other
than relegating that fly to hat-decorating duty.

Poor storage ruins a lot of flies, especially dries, before they
ever get used. The main problem is crushing, either by the lid on a
container that's too shallow or overstuffed, or by the rough handling
required to get the fly in and out of the container.

You can get fly wallets and boxes with all kinds of fancy padding,
styrofoam, magnets and hook clips. For my money, though, a fly box
with large, deep compartments is hard to beat.

The worst place of all to store flies is on the lamb's-wool patch on your vest. Dry flies get crushed, and barbless hooks fall out. A patch full of big, gaudy streamers is for theatrical effect.

After trout, trees, rocks and sleight-of-hand artists, the biggest threat to your flies is moisture. Always dry them soon after use—not on the vest patch, but at home on the mantel or dresser top. Just leave the box lid open, and keep the cat and parakeet away.

Moths and bugs can wreak havoc, too. If you've got a supply of flies stored up, watch for tiny tooth marks. Have an army of moth balls ready.

Steaming often can revive bedraggled dry-fly hackle. Grasp the hook bend with forceps and hold the fly over a teapot spout. When the hackle's fluffed back out, stand the fly on its eye until it's dry.

TO CATCH A TROUT,
YOU'VE GOT TO THINK LIKE A TROUT

CUTE, but pure baloney. If you tried to think like a trout, you couldn't find one hand with the other.

Instead of thinking, as in "reasoning," trout only react to stimuli in their environment. Even a fungus can do that.

Trout react to their surroundings in only two ways—successfully and unsuccessfully. If they react successfully, they survive, grow and pass on their genes to the next generation. If they react unsuccessfully, they die, even in the absence of anglers. Most die young. A few don't.

Sounds grim, and indeed it is for the trout. For you, though, it's a perception of biological reality around which to build your angling strategies.

The challenge the trout presents is threefold. First, you must learn to recognize the stimuli beyond your control which act on the trout and cause it to react in certain ways. Second, you must avoid creating stimuli which are likely to put it off its feed. Finally, you must create stimuli which fool it into taking your fly.

Work at mastering these skills, and you'll survive and grow as a trout angler. The matter of successfully passing on your genes to the next generation is best left for another book.

BROWN TROUT

WHERE DO THE TROUT HANG OUT?

TROUT that react successfully don't make life any harder on themselves than necessary. The secret of finding them is to look for places you might be if you were a trout. Limber up your fins, now, and come a-long. You're going to learn to behave like a trout.

Because you'll be most interested in adult fish as an angler, we'll pretend you've already finned your way through childhood and adolescence. Many of your needs and preferences were different then.

Now your basic functions in life are to survive, feed and reproduce. That's all. Survival comes first.

To do it, you'll need several things—enough water to cover your back, enough oxygen to keep your metabolism going, refuge when danger threatens and plenty of food you don't have to work too hard to get. Others of your kind are looking for the same things, so you'll have to compete with them.

All else being equal, you'll prefer deep water for the protection it provides from herons, raccoons and other predators. Any depth over two feet is enough. Shallower than that and you'll be there for some other reason—perhaps the food supply is better or maybe you've been crowded out of the deeper spots.

Trout aren't territorial, as some people have claimed, but they do set up a definite pecking order. The biggest ones claim the best feeding spots, and the rest get what's left. Interestingly, though, fear temporarily breaks down the pecking order, and trout all hiding in the same place treat each other very democratically till the danger's past.

Chasing food burns up a lot of energy, so you'll want to find a spot where the food comes to you, instead. The most likely place is in the current, where a lot of dislodged or emerging insects and sick or injured baitfish get swept by. All you have to do is sit there and pick from the passing smorgasbord.

You'll use up a lot of energy just staying put if you wait directly in the main flow. Instead, you'll want to wait in the slower water on the edge of the main current where you can dart out and grab things as they come by. Or maybe you can find a small pocket of slow water surrounded by the main current on all sides. It only needs to be as large as yourself. Look behind, or just in front of, a rock or log. Maybe you can find a little depression in the bottom where the worst of the current goes overhead. The current's always slowest on the bottom, and you'll spend most of your time there. If you're a brown trout, you'll usually seek out slower water than you would if you were a rainbow.

As long as there's no danger threatening, you'll not worry much about venturing out in the open and into the shallows for food. You may even snake over the gravel with your back exposed if the prey is worth the effort. Scuds sometimes congregate at the water's edge by the hundreds of thousands in the spring, and you can scoop them up by the bucketful.

You didn't reach adulthood by being a hero. The slightest hint of danger will send you fleeing for cover. Your ancestors invented the old cliche about discretion being the better part of valor. You'll prefer to get under a log, a rock or a cutbank if you can. If there's none available, you may try to blend in with the side of something. If all else fails, you'll just head for deep water and hope.

A few of your kind move up and down the stream quite a bit, but most live out their lives within a couple hundred feet of their first home. Usually, you'll just hunker down in an eddy when it floods, but a few of your brethren may head upstream. Only the dead and dying get swept downstream.

One vital aspect of your environment is water temperature. It affects you profoundly, because you're a cold-blooded animal. Too cold, and your metabolism slows down and reduces your feeding rate. You won't die, but you won't grow much, either. Too warm and you burn up calories like crazy. At first, you'll go into a feeding frenzy. With luck, you might take in as much energy as you burn up. Soon, though, you won't be able to get enough oxygen to sustain your feverish activity, even if there's plenty in the water. If you don't cool off soon, your future is bleak.

With luck, you'll know of a cool spring or seep nearby and head for it. Otherwise, you'll just sit tight and suffer.

Assuming the water's cold enough, there's only one place in Missouri where you'll have to worry about enough dissolved oxygen. That's at the upper end of Lake Taneycomo where oxygen-poor water from the depths of Table Rock Lake is discharged through the dam from mid-September into early December. If you're there, you'll be in a stupor much of the time.

Although a shortage of oxygen will seldom be a problem, you'll often avoid many spring pools and upper spring branches because of the water's high nitrogen and carbon dioxide content. It can give you the bends, just like deep-sea divers get. If you do venture there, it'll most likely be in winter or early spring when the gas content usually is least.

MIND YOUR MANNERS

WITH MORE PEOPLE stalking Missouri's trout waters each year, good man-
ners are essential for everyone's fishing pleasure and success.
   One of the most boorish kinds of behavior is to crowd in on other
people and cast across their lines. A habit spawned in the trout
parks where crowding is often unavoidable, the only reasons for it
elsewhere are ignorance and rudeness. Don't be a jerk—the world already has enough of those. 'Nuff said.
   Unlike other methods, fly fishing requires backcasting room. There
are two ways to pass by another fly caster. The simplest is to circle
around out of his backcast's reach. If that's not possible, pause
until he's laid his cast on the water, say, "Comin' behind," and hurry
on by. He'll appreciate your courtesy, and you'll be spared the
trouble of extracting a hook from your ear, or worse.

Highbanking is walking along or standing on top of the streambank in full view of the trout below. It's done only by amateurs and spectators, and there's no need for you to be either.

Highbanking isn't too serious during the summer season at the trout parks or at most of the fee areas. The trout there are fresh out of the hatchery and relatively unafraid. During the parks' winter season and elsewhere all year long, though, it's a great way to scare the wits out of the trout and give them lockjaw. If you must see what's at the bottom of the bank, get down on your hands and knees or crawl on your belly. Move slowly, and don't stick more than your nose over the top. For your own sake and everyone else's, don't highbank.

Noisy behavior such as splashy wading spooks stream-wise trout, too. Wade quietly and speak softly when you're near others, or where others will soon follow behind you. If you're canoeing past wading anglers, go behind them on the shallow side, if possible. If not, drift past rather than paddling. If you're the one who's wading, be sure to say, "Howdy" and "Thanks."

Some folks prefer to fish in solitude, and their wish should be respected. Most, though, enjoy a short streamside chat, and many life-long friendships have begun this way.

Relax and be yourself, with no fancy airs. Compliment others on their casting skill, equipment or flies. Few fly fishers can resist an opener like, "Boy, sure wish I could cast that well," or, "Nice rod —you build it?" Before long, you'll probably be in each other's fly boxes.

Always get permission before fishing on private property. Respect the fences, close the gates and leave the place cleaner than when you came. Don't take it personally if you're refused. Few landowners are selfish or mean. They've just had bad luck with other strangers who were.

Respect public property, too. You'd be appalled to know how many of your tax dollars are spent to repair the handiwork of vandals or others who are just plain thoughtless. The folks who work for public land agencies do their best, but they can't be everywhere all of the time. You can help fill the gap. Get involved.

Littering demeans the sport for everyone. If you brought it with you, it's even easier to take it back when you leave. There's no reason not to take someone else's litter back with you, too. That's a great use for the big pocket on the back of your fishing vest.

Never in its long history has the Conservation Commission passed a regulation because of malice or stupidity. Always abide by the regulations—not because you're supposed to, but because they help conserve the resource and provide better fishing for everyone. If the Commission has made an honest mistake, or if an experiment has failed, it'll become evident soon enough.

Few sights are more disgusting than an angler mucking up and down the stream with a rod in one hand and a beer in the other. If you enjoy an occasional streamside nip, do it with class. Find a comfortable log to relax on and pour yourself a finger or two in a battered old tin cup. Savor rather than guzzle. It's a great time to look for rises and hatches or to just admire the scenery.

One of the highest forms of fly-fishing etiquette is to teach a kid. Whether he or she is six or sixty, take one fishing every chance you get. Remember, someone took you once.

The gift that lasts a lifetime.

Finally, consider sharing most or all of your catch with others. Not at the supper table, but in the stream. A trout on your plate is a trout no one else will have the chance to catch. Releasing your fish for others to enjoy is not only good conservation, it's also a profound act of angling courtesy.

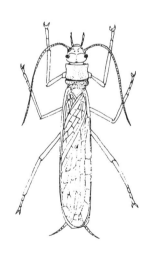

HERE WE GO

OKAY. You've got the equipment, and you know the basics of how to use it. You also know how the trout behave, and that's the first step in deceiving them. Somewhere in your fly box, there's one that should work. All you need now are practice, experience and less luck than you think. Let's go.

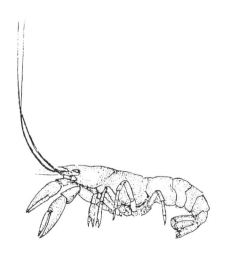

STALKING THE TROUT

STREAMSIDE. Your rod is strung, you've chosen the fly and tied it on, and you're full of enthusiasm. What next?

If you're like most Missouri trout anglers, you'll probably do one of two things. You may start walking along the top of the high bank looking for visible fish, or at least a fishy-looking spot.

"Ah—there's a big rock out there I can stand on. Prob'ly a big trout underneath it. I'll just let my fly drift under there and hang on tight. This is gonna be a snap."

Or you may enter the water on the shallow, low-bank side. No time to waste, so you splash your way out as far as you can wade. After all, the closer you can get to the fish, the easier it is to cast, right?

"Whoops. That cast didn't land just right—better pick it up and throw it again."

Well, if you're in one of the four trout parks, or one of the commercial fee-fishing areas, or anywhere else an hour after the stocking truck has left, you're probably doing okay. You couldn't scare those trout off their feed if you drove an army tank into the water.

But if you're anywhere else going after stream-wise trout, you've probably ruined any chance of catching a trophy or even a lot of smaller ones. Oh, you may pick up an occasional small fish, and perhaps that's good enough. More likely, you'll go home telling everybody the fishing was pretty poor. You may even be grousing that the stream's all fished out, and why doesn't the Conservation Department stock more fish?

There's a parody of an old cliche that says: "It may be better to light one little candle, but it's a whole lot more emotionally satisfying to curse the darkness." It never crosses your mind that it was your own clumsy behavior that gave the trout lockjaw all day long. Let's go back a few hours and do it a little better this time.

The Big Bright Butterfly Blunder

Your clumsy approach to the trout began before you ever left the house, when you put on that bright-red shirt you love so much. Sure makes you look classy, though, doesn't it? Just like Grizzly Adams.

Research has proven that trout do indeed see in color rather than black and white. Trout distinguish red most easily, followed by orange and yellow. They're least able to distinguish shades of blue and green. Unless you're willing to believe your red shirt looks like a big, bright butterfly to the trout, you'll do best to clothe yourself in drab colors that blend with the trout's natural world—green like the bushes, brown like the gravel bars, blue like the sky, and black or gray like the soil or a tree trunk.

Reconnoitering

Walking from your car to the water is a good time to scout out the situation. Is the water up or down? Clear or cloudy? Are any fish working the surface? Anything hatching? Lots od canoes, swimmers or other commotion? All these factors and more should influence your strategy when you finally reach the water. Fly choice is the last decision before the first cast.

The Art of Invisibility

Trout keep in touch with what's going on around them by the same ways that you and I do. They see, hear (sense vibrations), smell, feel and taste. Their most acute senses for detecting danger are sight and hearing. It follows, then, that you'll want to stay out of sight as best you can, or at least not look much different from your surroundings. You won't want to cause a lot of vibrations in the water, either.

Without going into the details of the trout's optical system and the refractive properties of water on light rays, the following table shows how far a trout can clearly distinguish the shape, color and movement of an out-of-the-water object if the water is clear and mirror-smooth. I got the information from Clarke and Goddard's The Trout and the Fly—a new approach. They got it from some very persuasive research.

Here's how far the trout can see you.

If a trout is this far beneath the water surface,	it can see an object this high above the water surface clearly from the indicated distance			
	4 feet above	5 feet above	6 feet abvve	7 feet above
2 feet	25 feet	31 feet	37 feet	42 feet
4 feet	28 feet	33 feet	39 feet	45 feet
6 feet	31 feet	37 feet	42 feet	49 feet

There are several ways to stay out of sight, or at least minimize the amount of you the fish can recognize. The first, of course, is to stand well back and make long casts, even laying much of your line on the gravel if necessary. That's not always possible, though, so we need to consider other ways, too.

One is to crawl or crouch low as you approach the water and to cast from a sitting or kneeling position. Another is to enter the water so less of you projects above the surface. Trout's underwater distance vision is surprisingly limited—perhaps no more than twenty feet—even in very clear water, so you're not trading a less-visible face for more-visible legs.

On small streams, you may also be able to conceal yourself behind trees, bushes, rocks or logs. Another way is to approach the trout from directly behind where its body blocks any vision. The ultimate way, of course, is to fish at night.

If you can't avoid exposing part of yourself either above or below the surface, moving very slowly and smoothly will make you less conspicuous than if you move with haste.

All of this presumes the water surface to be mirror-smooth. As it becomes more turbulent, light rays and the visual images they transmit become less coherent as they penetrate the surface. Thus, it's often possible to approach trout more closely in turbulent water than in smooth. You'll have to size up each situation as you come to it and behave accordingly.

The important points to remember are that stream-wise trout are a-fraid of you (you're a large potential predator; they're much smaller and potential prey), that they see you before you see them, and that invisible trout stalkers are often the most successful ones.

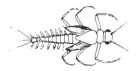

Invisibility Isn't Everything

Out of sight isn't necessarily out of mind. Another way you can ruin a great day or night of fishing is to behave noisily in the water. Out-of-the-water sounds don't penetrate the surface very effectively, so normal conversation and other noises of similar intensity don't matter much. It's the underwater sounds you'll have to guard against. You can't prevent them entirely, but you can minimize them.

The main rule is to wade slowly and deliberately. Some experts say that if you're rippling the surface ahead of you, you're wading too fast. Don't unnecessarily crunch and grind the gravel under your feet or clatter the rocks around too much. It can't help but improve your fishing success.

The last point involves both sound and sight. The question is when and how to pick up your cast for another one. Especially, what should you do with a bungled cast?

We've all watched fly casters beat the water to death trying to get a cast they're happy with. If you just want to exercise your arm, go ahead and do the same thing. But if you'd rather catch fish, all you're doing is ruining your chances.

Good cast or bad, the best technique is to not pick up until the line and fly have drifted out of where you think the trout are. You'll catch more fish for at least three reasons. First, you're not scaring them by constantly frothing the water. Moreover, your fly is in or on the water longer, instead of up in the air where only the birds, bats and trees can grab it. And finally, you're going to pick up an occasional trout from places where you didn't expect them to be.

THEORY AND PRACTICE OF WADING

WADING IS AN ESSENTIAL part of stream fishing because it gets you to where the trout lie. It's done best in an upright posture. With proper gear and sensible precautions, it can be as safe and enjoyable as hiking your favorite trail.

Staying Upright Rule No. 1: Always scout ahead before entering the water or changing location. That way, you'll never wade into a trap you can't get out of. Fix landmarks in your mind so you can retrace your path if necessary. Don't be a hero.

Staying Upright Rule No. 2: Never look directly at your feet. Instead, look ahead for the next safe spot to put them. Always keep your weight on the one that's firmly set till you're sure the other one's safe. Shuffle rather than step. If the flowing water starts to give you vertigo, concentrate your gaze on a stationary object like a tree well above waterline. Vertigo is unnerving at best and can lead to a dunking at worst.

Staying Upright Rule No. 3: Never tackle more current than you can safely handle. When crossing a stream in very swift water, angle down-and-across rather than straight across, if possible. Keep your feet well apart, with your side to the current to minimize your area of resistance. Put your arms out like a tightrope walker for balance. Look for slow water above or below logs and boulders, and use it. Use branches, logs and boulders for hand-holds, too.

A wading staff is an excellent aid for novices who feel unsure in the water. Experts use them, too, in heavy currents with slippery footing. Attach it to your waders or vest with a nylon cord. That way, both hands are free to cast, and it won't head for the Gulf of Mexico without you.

If you fail to heed the Staying Upright Rules, you'll need to know the How To Stay Alive Rules. First, always wear a wading belt snugly cinched around your wader top. If you go down or under, it'll keep the water out and the air in. The old wives' tale that you'll flip upside down and drown is sheer nonsense. Actually, the trapped air will help you float like a cork. Relax and drift or paddle to the nearest shallow water.

Waders full of water needn't drown you, either. The only extra weight you have to support is that of the waders themselves, not the water inside. If you're over your head and have trouble keeping your nose clear, alternately sink to the bottom, then spring back up, grabbing a breath of air each time your head clears the surface. You'll

find shallow water soon.
Waders won't drown you,
but panic will. If you
merely take a pratfall in
shallow water, wipe off
your injured dignity and
rise to fish again.

The last bits of advice
are the Staying Upright
Comfortably Rules: No. 1,
always wear enough socks
to prevent blisters; No.
2, always visit a thirsty
bush before putting on
your waders.

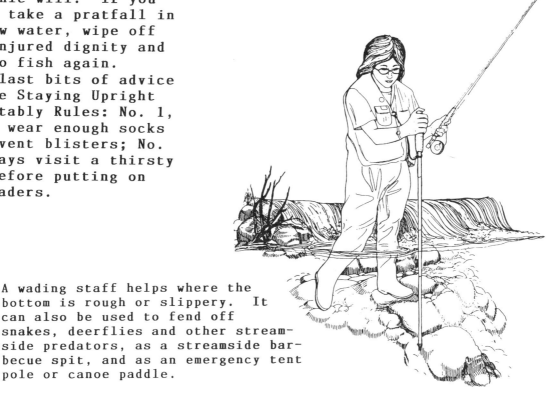

A wading staff helps where the
bottom is rough or slippery. It
can also be used to fend off
snakes, deerflies and other streamside predators, as a streamside bar-
becue spit, and as an emergency tent
pole or canoe paddle.

FLY PRESENTATION

PRESENTATION refers to how the fly is made to behave on or in the
water. Good presentation is any kind that fools the trout. Poor presentation is any kind they refuse.

Seems simple enough, but many folks—even some old timers—confuse
beautiful casting with perfect fly presentation. Everyone loves to
watch an expert caster's tight loops and arrow-straight delivery of
the fly to its target. Everyone, that is, except the trout. All they
care about is whether or not your fly looks and behaves like something
edible.

To the uninitiated, excellent presentation often looks like pretty
amateurish casting. There may be all kinds of bends, loops and wiggles in the line, or maybe it's piled in a heap around the fly. Done
unintentionally, there's no denying that it's not a very pretty sight.
Done on purpose to make the fly behave seductively, however, it's the
mark of a fly-fisher's skill. Beginners usually learn to cast beauti-
fully long before they learn to cast excellently.

There are many different kinds of behavior to be sought in a fly.
Often, an absolutely dead drift is most effective. At other times,
slight twitches interest the trout more. Occasionally, a fast, dart-
ing motion is best.

Flies can be presented at different depths, too. Nymphs are usually most successful when fished on or near the bottom. Emergers and many wet flies often are deadly when manipulated to rise from the bottom to the surface in front of the trout, a tactic called the Leisenring Lift, for its originator. Floating nymphs, pupae and stillborns usually are presented in or just under the surface film. Dries, of course, are presented on the water's surface.

When first offered to stream-wise trout, your fly should be manipulated to behave like the life form it represents, if any. The assumption, of course, is that both you and the trout agree on what your fly looks like. Undoubtedly, that's not always the case, so you might vary your presentation after a while if the original one doesn't work.

Your main adversary in making the fly behave as you wish is the current. Its troublesome effect works more on the line than on the fly. Want your nymph to drift freely on the bottom? The flow will grab your line and send it bellying downstream, dragging the fly under the surface behind it. Want your streamer to look like an injured minnow trying unsuccessfully to swim upstream? The current's drag on your line will shoot it headfirst downstream like the healthiest, most uncatchable meal in the river.

Because your fly must go where you think the trout are, it's the line that must be manipulated to overcome the current's infernal effects. There are many tactics to use. Here are several of the most important.

The snake cast, one way of laying slack line on the water.

Mending line

The most crucial move is in the execution of the cast. For drag-free drifts, you've got lay enough extra line on the water that it takes quite a while for the current to straighten out the slack and begin dragging the fly. That's why you'll often see the real experts' lines lying in wiggles, curves or piles. Vince Marinaro's "puddle" cast (In the Ring of the Rise, Crown, 1976, ISBN 0-517-52550-X) looks wretched on the water, but you can dead-drift a dry fly over Niagara Falls with it. To get a nymph or streamer on the bottom before the current drags it back to the surface, try George Harvey's "tuck" cast. It's described in Joe Humphreys' book, Trout Tactics (Stackpole, 1981, ISBN 0-8117-2079-0). Other types of slackline casts also are effective, far more so than the traditionally beautiful kind.

Once your cast is committed to the water, the most common way to overcome or at least delay drag is by "mending" line. In this maneuver, a semicircular motion of the rod tip is used to flip the dragging line section up or downstream, whichever is needed to keep the fly on its desired course. It can't be done with a full-sinking line, and it's only partially effective with a sinking tip.

Another technique is to follow the direction of the line's float with your rod tip, rather than holding it stationary. You may want to feed extra line off the reel sometimes, too.

The traditional cast for a dead-drift presentation is made either directly or slanting upstream. Line is then retrieved at the same rate the fly drifts back toward you.

A more difficult but often deadlier method is a downstream slackline cast followed by releasing line or lowering the rod tip at the same rate the fly is drifting away from you. That way, the trout sees the fly before the leader and line. A drawback is that setting the hook sometimes pulls the fly straight back out of the trout's mouth. The trick is to delay the hook-set for an extra micro-instant (it'll just seem like an eternity) until the fish turns to restation itself, thereby driving the hook into the side or corner of its mouth.

Active fly presentations can be made in any direction, depending mostly on how near the bottom you want to get. Casting well upstream from the trout's lie allows time for the fly to sink before you set it into motion. An across or down-and-across delivery will work the fly at shallower depth.

Most of the time, you'll want your fly to strike the water softly. There are two exceptions to this generality, though. One is with big terrestrial imitations like grasshoppers which often land on the water quite noisily in real life. In this case, trout often recognize a loud "splat" as the sign of a sizeable meal, rather than as a portent of danger. The other is where a trout can be reached only from behind. In this case, splatting the fly slightly to its rear may catch its attention rather than scare it. It'll spin around, take the fly without much inspection and immediately wheel back to its lie. It's exciting when it works, and nothing's lost if it doesn't.

Fly-fishing literature is replete with descriptions of trout foods and the behavioral patterns of their different life stages. One of the best summaries of this information is Dave Whitlock's Guide to Aquatic Trout Foods (Winchester Press, 1982, ISBN 0-87691-377-0). In it, Dave also explains fly-presentation techniques to imitate each life stage. It's mandatory reading for the serious trout stalker.

WHY DO TROUT TAKE A FLY?

NO ONE but Doctor Doolittle has ever conversed intelligently with a trout, but experience suggests three reasons. The most obvious one, of course, is hunger; the fly is mistaken for a natural food. This is the theory behind imitations.

Another is curiosity. Your fly may not resemble a familiar food very much, but it looks or acts like something good enough to eat. Lacking hands, the only way the trout can find out is to chomp down on it. This is the theory behind attractors.

The third is harder to hang a name on, but I'll call it annoyance or aggressiveness. Waggle the right kind of fly in a trout's face long enough, and it'll sometimes attack to defend its place in the stream-bottom pecking order or just to get rid of the darn thing.

WHY DON'T TROUT TAKE A FLY?

FOR A LOT MORE reasons than why they do. Lack of hunger is the least
of them. Trout are animated feeding machines and can gorge themselves
to astounding lengths when the pickin's are easy.

The most obvious reason, of course, is that they recognize your fly
as bogus because of its appearance or behavior. Equally important is
that you may have frightened them by your appearance or commotion.

Your fly may be too far away or moving too fast. The energy required to capture it would be more than the energy they could digest from
it if it were real. Trout that fail to learn this lesson lose at the
game of life, even in the absence of hooks.

Although trout usually are opportunists and take anything edible
that comes along, there are times when they become maddeningly selective. Most often, this happens during a major hatch, when the water's
alive with specimens of one particular insect. Trout key in on a dis-
tinguishing feature of that insect and respond only to it, probably to
avoid the energy expenditure required to check out a variety of other
possible but unproven morsels. If your fly doesn't imitate what
they've keyed in on, you're out of luck. This is why fly fishers try
to match the hatch.

Trout go off their feed in response to extreme water temperatures,
too. Too cold, and their metabolism slows down to a snail's pace.
Too warm, and they're in a stupor near death.

I'll not go into changes in the weather, phases of the moon or any
other theories and old wives' tales. In my limited experience, they
fail about as often as they succeed. Besides, what would you have
left to argue about if I did?

NOTHING'S HAPPENING—NOW WHAT?

YOU'VE BEEN CASTING for an hour, maybe more, with no luck. The challenge now is to reach into your bag of tricks and come up with a winner. What to try next? Here are some possibilities.

Move on to the next good-looking spot. Perhaps there aren't any fish where you are. If there are, maybe they aren't feeding, or maybe you or someone else has spooked them.

Stay where you are, but give the water a rest. If you've spooked the fish, that'll give them time to calm down and come back on the feed again.

Whether you travel on or stay put, move more stealthily. Clumsy approaches probably give more trout lockjaw than any other single thing. Stay low, sneak up from behind, back off farther, and move slower and more quietly.

Try casting more softly. Maybe the slap of your line on the water is scaring the daylights out of them. Many folks try to cast farther than their skill allows. Shorten up. Cast between wind gusts instead of into their teeth.

Present the fly differently. If a dead drift isn't working, twitch it a little. With big streamers, try a faster or slower strip or no action at all.

If you're using anything but a dry fly, try presenting it at a different depth. Most trout usually lie near the bottom, and they're often reluctant to move very far for food. Trout that use more energy chasing food than they digest from it don't live long. If they're still there, they've learned better.

Keep the same fly pattern, but change to a different size. If they look at what you've got but won't take it, try the next size smaller. If you don't have one, trim the big one down with clippers. If that doesn't work, try going up several sizes in hopes that a larger meal will entice them.

If there's an insect hatch in progress, try to match it. You don't have to know the insect's name, just what it looks like. If you can't match it exactly, try the nearest fly you've got to it. If that fails, try the emerger instead of the dry or vice versa. If that fails, too, look for another insect you may not have noticed at first. If all else fails, try to break through the hatch with a big, juicy attractor that's just too good to pass up.

Try a different fly pattern. Trout sometimes get finicky even when there isn't a hatch on.

Try a longer leader and a longer, smaller tippet. Actually, trout probably see the leader and tippet just as well as we do. But the less conspicuous they are in comparison to the fly, the better your chances are.

Try a different kind of water. If you can't find them in the pools, try the riffles or vice versa. If they're not out in the open, crowd the cover more closely.

Move closer to the springs that feed the stream. Everyone knows the water's cooler there in the summer, but it's also warmer there in the winter. Missouri's springwater temperature of about 58 degrees is perfect for trout year 'round.

Try a different time of day. In summer, warm water may make them lethargic in late afternoon. Try dawn, dusk or dark instead. In the winter, water temperature may be best in late afternoon. Browns and rainbows feed most actively between about fifty-two and sixty-eight degrees.

If things get really desperate, try another stream if there's one nearby. It may be cooler or warmer or lower or any number of other things in your favor.

If nothing works, go drown your sorrows in a chocolate milkshake or a beautiful sunset.

Above all else, always try again tomorrow.

STRIKE!

ANGLING'S most decisive moment is the instant of the strike. Unlike using live bait, fishing with the fly doesn't afford the luxury of waiting while the trout nibbles or carries off your bogus meal to a safer dining place. You've got to detect the strike instantly and re-act before the deception is discovered and spit out. There's little margin for error.

If you're drifting or stripping streamers or wet flies across-current or downstream on a tight line, you'll usually feel the strike as a sharp tug almost instantly. Sometimes, the strike's force alone will drive the hook home. At other times, you'll need to set the hook yourself. You don't need to give the rod a gargantuan heave with your entire body; just lift the tip swiftly but deliberately with your arm. The hook will penetrate easily if it's well honed, and your tippet will stay in one piece.

The process is a little trickier when drifting dry or almost-dry flies on a slackline cast. In this case, strikes at and just beneath the surface must be seen rather than felt. They'll vary from a small dimple or swirl to a powerful leap in the air, with everything in between. Usually, the fly will be taken on the trout's way up, but occasionally it'll be taken on the way back down.

When your sunken fly is taken by an unseen trout swirling beneath the surface, set the hook swiftly but deliberately as before. If any part of the trout shows above the surface, however, wait an extra micro-instant till it's headed back toward the bottom before setting the hook. Striking back the instant the fish appears or while it's still in the air likely will pull the fly out of its mouth before its jaws have closed. We all get buck fever and pull the trigger too soon every now and then, but cool nerves put more trout in the net.

Dead-drifting a deep nymph or wet fly on an upstream cast presents the ultimate challenge in strike detection. The tactic here is to concentrate intently on the end of your floating line where it attaches to the leader, or on the point where your sinking-tip line dives beneath the surface. Set the hook swiftly at the slightest pause or the minutest twitch at these points. Sometimes it'll only be a rock or root, but most often it'll be a trout. If you wait for a tug or other sharp line movement before reacting, you'll not hook many fish.

Strike detectors can help you recognize these subtle takes. Some are small fluorescent chartreuse or orange adhesive strips you can stick to the end of your line. A small tuft of bright yarn knotted on your line works, too. Some floating lines have a bright-orange tip built in. Most sinking-tip lines have a brightly colored floating section that ends where the darker sinking section begins.

Wood, cork, plastic and styrofoam bobbers are not strike detectors. They're bobbers, and ne'er the twain shall meet.

OMIGOSHIVEGOTWUN—WADOIDONOW?

IT'S ON. Now what?

For many, it's the ultimate rush in fly fishing—that magical, fleeting instant when you sense the trout is on. Doubts and dreams simultaneously flood your mind. Is it THE big one? Or just a little fella? Is it on securely or just barely nicked?

"I've already lost a couple today. Sure hope I don't lose this one, too. Oh, Lord! It's headed for the brush. Aaugh!"

Let's face it—you're not going to land them all, even the little
ones. But you'll land a lot more if you know what to do next.

Your first move is to get the rod tip high, somewhere between forty-
five and seventy-five degrees from the water surface. If the tip is
lower than forty-five degrees, the rod can't flex enough to absorb
the shock of a fast run. Ping! There goes your tippet.

"Nuts."

If your rod tip is higher than about seventy-five degrees, you're a
dead duck if the trout runs straight at you. Talk about helpless—
you've never seen so much slack line everywhere.

With your rod tip high, the second fleeting instant is only slightly
longer than the first. Through some sort of mystical instinct, you
have to decide what you're up against. With luck, the trout is doing
the same thing, making some tentative moves or just lying there like a
rock, testing you. Otherwise, it's trying to be somewhere else out
of sheer panic. Exciting, if it doesn't break off, disappointing if
it does.

You have two basic options to bring it in. If you judge in that
second fleeting instant that it's just a little fella that presents no
threat to your tippet, you can probably strip the line in with your
free hand. If the rod's in your right hand, pull in a foot or two of
line with your left. Clasp it beneath the forefinger of your rod hand
each time you pull in a section. If the trout makes a stronger-than-
expected run, give it some line by easing up the pressure of your
forefinger.

Many fly fishers, even old-timers, play fish this way all their
lives—even big ones. They land a lot, too, maybe even most. But
they also lose a lot, unnecessarily.

Playing big or even medium-sized trout by hand is strictly for novices. The human mind and muscle system simply can't vary line tension fast enough by adjusting finger pressure alone.

The experts, and anyone can be one in this respect, play all but the
smallest trout off the reel. When the fish isn't offering much resistance, reel it in just as if you were using a casting or spinning rod.
If it makes a stronger run than you can safely resist, just let go of
the reel handle and let the drag keep tension on the line. One of fly
fishing's most exciting experiences is the sound of the reel drag
chattering as a trout makes a powerful run.

The main trick to master in playing fish off the reel is getting
your slack line taken in soon after the strike. There are several
options. The simplest, which usually is adequate, is to hold the rod
tip high so line-guide friction keeps tension between you and the
trout. Then, just reel in the slack.

The second option combines a high rod tip with the line held lightly under the forefinger of your rod hand for a little extra tension.
A variation is to also run the slack line through a crook in the little finger of your rod hand so the line winds more tightly onto the
reel. You'll fumble around at first, but eventually you'll develop
your own style.

Another way to vary line tension when a trout runs is to vary the
angle of the rod to the line. If you point the rod straight at the
fish, your line is parallel to the rod and there's little friction on
it as it speeds through the guides. On the other hand, a vertical rod
creates a lot of friction as the line travels through the guides. Un-

less you're trying to steer the trout in a particular direction, keep the rod high most of the time.

Most trout react to the hook by heading for the swiftest current or nearest cover. Your strategy should be to get it into shallower, slower water as quickly as possible. There, it can't break you off in the brush or use the current's force against you.

One mistake is made more often than any other at this point. That's trying to steer the trout from swift water or cover with the rod held upright. A good fish can fight you to a standoff for a long time that way. The longer the fight goes on, the better the trout's chances of escaping.

Instead, steer it by holding your rod parallel to the water surface and away from your side at ninety degrees to the line. You'll be a-mazed at how much more effective this is.

Many experts recommend that you play fish with your strongest arm. Of course, that's your casting arm. In this case, the reel should be mounted so the handle is accessible to your other hand.

An alternative used by many fine fly fishers is to mount the reel so you can transfer the rod to your weaker arm and reel with the better-coordinated hand. The choice is yours.

One of the fly fisher's greatest moments of hysteria is when a hooked trout charges straight toward him. No matter how you try, you simply can't strip or reel in fast enough to keep line tension between you and the fish. There's slack line everywhere—in your lap, in your hands and all over the water. Now what?

There's only one thing to do. Keep the rod tip high and bring in line as fast as possible. If you're trying to get it onto the reel, abandon that idea and start stripping it in like fury. Head for shore as fast as you can. If you're already on the shore, head for the trees or any other direction that'll put distance between you and the trout. As soon as you get line tension back, return to the water and play the fish normally.

One of the most fascinating, challenging and nerve-wracking things about fly fishing is that you must handle your gear in a way that causes the fish to tire itself to the point where it can be eased in. Too little pressure, and it'll swim around forever, eventually dying from exhaustion. Too much pressure, and it'll break off. Mastery is somewhere in between.

If you've grown up with a casting or spinning rod, you'll probably have a couple of old habits to break. One is a tendency to muscle your trout in as rapidly as you can overpower it. Except for very small ones, this just isn't possible with fly-fishing tackle. Try it, and you'll have flies and tippet swimming all over the river.

The other old habit is planting your feet in concrete and playing your fish from one spot. With a fly rod, you'll need to follow bigger fish up and downstream as they run.

That's enough to get you started. You're going to do some fumbling around. You're going to lose some trout, but you're going to land some, too. Whichever happens, you'll be a bit better each time.

Read voraciously. Never hesitate to ask questions. There's a special bond among fly fishers that makes them spill their guts at the drop of a hat. Experiment, too.

Relish the triumphs and laugh off the failures. Above all, fish as often as you can. You won't catch trout if your fly isn't in the water.

NETTING YOUR TROUT

YOU'VE SENSED the trout is ready to bring in. Careful, now. Many fine fish are lost just as they reach the net.

Inexperienced anglers and excitable veterans often grab their net too soon. The result is a fish swimming circles around them just out of reach. Worse yet, they're trying to do three things with only two hands—hold the rod, hold the net and bring in more line.

Rather than trying to gauge how near the trout is to you, estimate the length of line and leader between it and the rod tip. If it's much greater than the length of the rod, bring in more line. If possible, leave the line-to-leader junction off the rod tip so that any bulge or roughness there won't hang up in the tip guide if the fish makes an unexpected run.

Okay. You've finally got the fish-to-rod-tip distance right, and the fish is fairly calm. What next?

Some folks try to sneak or swoop the net up from behind and catch the fish tail-first. This sometimes works, but usually it's a poor tactic. Fish can sense the commotion behind them and often will spurt away with exasperating speed.

Most properly tired fish will come in either upright or on their side. The best strategy is to hold the net rim motionless a few inches beneath the water surface and draw the fish over it, head-first. Then lift, and it's yours.

Be on guard, though, against a sudden flurry when the fish first spies the net. If it happens, be cool. Give line if you must, and start over. Above all, don't make a desperate lunge for it. Desperation seldom works, and often depletes your fly supply by one.

LANDING YOUR TROUT WITHOUT A NET

MANY TROUT, even fair-sized ones, can be landed safely without a net. Your first decision is whether you're going to keep or release it.

If it's going in the creel, it won't matter how badly you injure it so long as there's no chance it can get away, only to die later.

The easiest way is to beach it on the nearest gravel bar. Hold the rod a little above parallel to the ground and ninety degrees away from the fish. Don't try to drag it out of the water like a log. Instead, just maintain firm line tension. As the trout enters the shallows and feels the bottom, it'll start flopping. With each flop, your line tension will bring it a little closer. Soon, it'll be well up on the shore where you can pounce on it.

If you're not in a beaching situation, grasp the fish from above with your thumb and fingers pressed tightly over the rear of the gill covers. Strike fast and squeeze hard. It takes some practice.

There probably are a hundred ways definitely not to land a trout, whether you intend to keep it or not. One of the most common is to grab it around the middle and squeeze. Chances are, it'll spurt out of your hand like a bar of soap. Another you've seen in the fishing magazines or on TV is to pick it up by the lower jaw with your thumb in its mouth. That may immobilize bass, but it doesn't do a thing to trout except give them a lot of freedom to wriggle loose. Don't try this on brown trout, especially. Those razor teeth will turn your thumb to hamburger.

I hope you'll choose to release many or most of your trout. If so, you'll want to treat them as gently as possible so they can live to be caught again.

You may not believe this next method until you've tried it. Just cradle your hand gently under the trout's chest and lift. It'll lie there almost forever as long as you hold it perfectly upright and don't squeeze. I'm not sure why, but it's probably because you're supporting the fish's internal organs in their natural position rather than squashing them around. Try it. It really does work.

The ultimate method of harmlessly landing trout you intend to release doesn't even require touching them. First, fool them with a barbless hook. Then, just reach under the water, grasp the hook with your fingers or forceps, and twist or back it out. Nothin' to it.

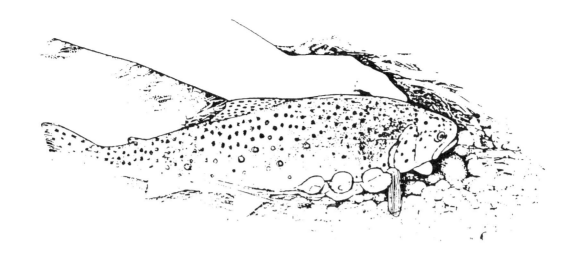

REVIVING AND RELEASING

GOOD. You've decided to release this one. Maybe it's undersized or you've already creeled as many as you can sensibly use or it's your way of conserving the resource. Whatever the reason, you'll want to do it right so the trout can live to fight again.

The most common way of releasing a trout is to wrestle it from the net, tear the hook out, rub off all its protective mucus and heave it back into the water. The overhand pitch is fairly uncommon. More often, you'll see variations of the underhand lob. Some folks keep it simple; others like to see how many times the fish can end-over-end before it hits the water. An added flourish is to let it slip free and bash on the rocks first.

There's a better way.

Actually, the whole process begins the instant the hook drives home. Play the fish as hard as the tackle will allow, bring it to the net as quickly as possible and land it gently.

If it's in the net, there's no need to grab it to remove the fly. Just reach in, work the hook free and drop it into the water beside you. Admire your capture for a moment, say something appreciative to it, then dip your net into the water and nudge it out. Be sure to make the release in slow water rather than the swift current.

If it bolts away instantly, feel good about yourself. It may just sit there, regaining its strength and sense of direction. Don't force it away. It'll leave when it's ready.

If it starts to belly up, you've got some work to do. Grasp its tail between your thumb and forefinger. If it's a big one, cradle it under its chest, too. Hold it level and upright, face to the flow so it can reorient itself and feed lots of oxygen-laden water past its gills. If the current is sluggish, move the trout forward and back to create an artificial one. Don't give up too soon. I've spent up to several minutes reviving some fish, and it was time well invested.

Research has shown that skillfully played, revived and released trout generally have a ninety percent or better chance of surviving with no ill effect. Handled poorly, though, their chances can plummet to fifty percent or less. One of the best marks of a fly-fishing expert is the skill with which he revives and releases his prey.

THE TALKING TACTIC

IF YOU'RE LIKE MOST FOLKS, talking to yourself and your quarry is an indispensable part of fly-fishing strategy. Be cunning during the stalk.

"Come on, now. I know you're there. Eeeasy. Gotcha!" Who can deny the intellectual intensity of conversation like that?

Once the trout is on, the action picks up fast. "Whoooah! Get outta there. Come to Daddy (or Momma), now. Steeeady. Awright!"

Always take a moment to admire your capture, be it large or small. "Lordy, aren't you a pretty thing. Just look at those spots!" If you don't feel at least a little twinge of reverence, you're probably in the wrong sport.

At this point, your trout undoubtedly is scared out of its wits. Calm its fears with, "Easy, big guy. You'll be back home in just a second. There you go. See ya next time."

To the uninitiated, all this sounds a little silly or downright dumb. Don't worry. The rest of us know it's love talk, and that's all that really matters.

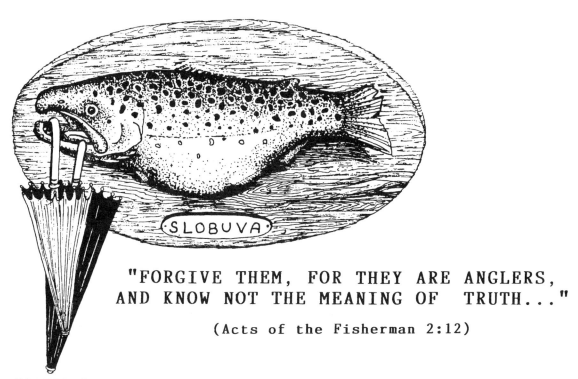

"FORGIVE THEM, FOR THEY ARE ANGLERS,
AND KNOW NOT THE MEANING OF TRUTH..."

(Acts of the Fisherman 2:12)

BOASTING, leg stretching, rib tickling and knee slapping are among angling's greatest pleasures. Who could ever doubt a story like, "Harry, ya shoulda been there! This slobuva brown savaged my size-28 Thunder Wing like it was the last bug on earth, see..." Not me, for sure.

Now that you're on a roll, always be sure that Ol' Slobuva was captured under the most impossible circumstances imaginable. "Remember when the big wind blew Old Man Smedley's outhouse in the branch last year? Well, Ol' Slobuva was lyin' right behind the seat just like he was peerin' through a porthole. Had to snake my cast around the water gate and under the roof so it'd float right in the door. May lightning strike me dumb, Harry—I'll swear I seen an angel carry my line across the water and drop it there."

Around the campfire, monster trout are always subdued with spider-weblike tippet, too. Casually mention something like, "Little fella made off with the last of my tippet in the pool below. Rummaged around in the bottom of my pouch and found an old tangled-up piece left over from years ago. Ugly sight, all fulla wind knots and such. Scraped off the moss 'n' mold, and cinched it on. Musta been 8 or 10X, I'd judge."

Legendary trout should also have heroic physical features that set them apart from the rest of the crowd. "Harry, ya shoulda seen the hook-jaw on that thing. Coulda used it for a bumbershoot hanger down at the lodge on a frog-strangler Saturday night, and had room left over. Gut on him like he'd et a cannonball. Only one fin, too. Dunno what happened to the others. Maybe lost 'em comin' through the old grist mill. Fightin' off the young bucks while courtin' the ladies, more likely. He'd a weighed twice as much if he'd had all his parts. Oh, he's seen a thing or two in his time, you betcha."

As long as you're at it, you might as well add a couple inches and half a pound or so to Ol' Slobuva. Harry's going to subtract at least that much, no matter how sincere you sound!

FISHING THE FOUR SEASONS

EACH SEASON adds its own dimension to the Missouri trout-fishing experience. Spring brings that rebirth of hope called Opening Day at the trout parks. Undaunted by high water and the fury of the elements, thousands return each March 1 to revel in this madcap adventure.

Among those who prefer more quiet waters, the event goes almost unnoticed. Caddisflies are waking from their pupal slumber, and dry-fly fishing soon will be at its best. The Hendricksons erupt in April, and the Light Cahills follow soon after. Big streamers and nymphs worked deep are often deadly. The air is sweet, the breezes soft, the streamsides carpeted with wildflowers. The fly-fisher's life is good then.

Summer brings crowds to many trout waters and heat to them all. On the larger streams, the aluminum (canoe) hatch is in full swing.

Many anglers stoically accept this turn of events, but others change their tactics. Some retreat to smaller, lesser-known waters, especially on the weekends. The days are long, and many cast only in the morning's mist or evening's shadows, when the world is cooler and less hectic. The adventurous work big streamers in the darkness for monster browns that come out to prowl. Summer is wonderful, too.

Fall brings serenity and heady scents on the wind. The crowds have slackened, and the hills are ablaze with autumn. The days are crisp, the nights nippy. Grasshoppers clatter in the grass, and many fall prey to hungry trout. Many of summer's hatches persist into November, and cooler water once again puts fish on the rise. For many trout stalkers, this is the finest season of all.

Winter is the undiscovered season, and that's a shame. The trout parks, which closed at the end of October, re-open in mid-November for the catch-and-release season. It's an experience no one should miss. At Lake Taneycomo, the stout of heart gather below Table Rock Dam and cast to big browns and rainbows on their annual runs upstream.

Elsewhere, most of the streams are nearly deserted, except for the few hardy souls who cherish the solitude and good fishing. With a Thermos of hot coffee in your vest, winter can be a special time on Missouri's trout waters.

TROUT CONSERVATION

NO MATTER where you stalk Missouri's trout, your pleasure and success depend on conservation.

Most people have assumed that public and private hatcheries could produce an endless supply of trout. No need to worry about taking them out of the water at your end, somebody's always putting more in at the other.

Also, most people have thought the big Ozark springs that supply most of Missouri's trout water would always flow icy-clear and unpolluted. No problem there—the springwater comes from some mysterious, far-away place, and it's purified by filtering through soil and rock.

Until recently, the first perception has been fairly true. The latter never has been. Neither will be in the future.

Let's take a look at the trout supply first. Trout for public waters come from state hatcheries at Bennett Spring, Montauk Spring, Maramec Spring, Roaring River and Branson, from the federal hatchery at Neosho, and from other federal hatcheries at Norfolk and Greers Ferry, Arkansas. Trout for privately controlled waters come from commercial hatcheries near Gravois Mills, Cassville, Steelville, Ava and Rockbridge.

In a dozen or more streams, rainbows perpetuate themselves naturally. Brown trout spawn, but their eggs fail to survive, presumably because Missouri waters are too warm during the November spawning season.

Big rainbows making little ones.

Commercial hatchery production undoubtedly fluctuates with the law of supply and demand. The eventual limiting factor will be the number of springs economically suitable for present hatchery expansion and new hatchery development. Several of the smallest private hatcheries have gone out of business in recent years.

Although the Conservation Department is in the early stages of bolstering its hatchery-production capability, the increase will be modest, and it won't happen overnight.

With more anglers on these waters each year, there are only three known ways to maintain the trout resource for everyone's benefit. The first is to restrict the creel limit and return fish to the water so they can grow larger and be caught several times instead of just once.

The second is to restrict the use of natural baits in favor of artificial lures and flies. Again, scientific research has proven that trout caught with artificials usually are hooked less deeply and survive better when released than those taken on natural baits. Cutting the leader and leaving deeply lodged hooks in rather than tearing them out helps, but the mortality rate still is ten times greater than for lightly hooked fish. Neither of these approaches will put more trout in the frying pan, but both can help provide good sport for more people.

The last way can help provide more trout for both the sport and table. Conservation Department research indicates that rainbows probably can reproduce naturally in many more streams than at present if enough are allowed to reach maturity before they're caught and kept. At least three years, often four, are necessary for streambred rainbows to reach spawning age.

The single greatest obstacle to all of these solutions is the human reluctance to return fish to the water so they can grow, spawn and be caught again. Still, no one has offered any better solutions at an affordable price. Although it won't happen overnight, anglers increasingly will be asked to abide by smaller creel limits, larger length limits and less use of natural baits.

Missouri's public waters have the potential for unsurpassed trout-fishing sport, but they just can't feed the entire trout-eating world forever. You can help by supporting regulations which protect and improve this precious resource. Don't do it for the fish—do it for yourself.

No two things are more closely tied than trout and clean water. If there was ever any question that Ozark trout waters could be polluted, the fish kill at Maramec Spring in 1981 settled it once and for all. The incident was caused by a pipeline break which leaked ammonia into porous soil and bedrock thirteen miles away. Seeping and flowing through subterranean passageways, the lethal liquid emerged from the spring less than two weeks later.

Although most Ozark springs draw their flow from more modest distances, some of the largest are known to be fed from more than forty miles away. The same thing could happen to them, large or small. The Ozark soil and bedrock simply are too porous to provide the kind of water purification that people would like to believe in.

Other causes of water pollution may be less dramatic, but they're just as destructive. Municipal and industrial wastes, septic-tank leachates, clouds of mud from eroding land and instream gravel dredging, and removal of water-cooling streamside shade—all are threats to trout and our happy pursuit of them.

Habitat destruction by channelization, dredging and streambank cattle grazing are serious threats, too. If the Almighty had meant cows, bulldozers and draglines to be in trout streams, He would have given them fins.

You can play a vital role in water-quality and habitat protection. Your first duty is to be alert. Your second is to be well-informed. Righteous indignation won't buy you a cup of coffee if you don't know the details of what's happening or what you're talking about.

Your worst source of information often is yourself. The second worst usually is your fishing buddies. The third is a newsstand outdoor magazine.

The rainbow's end

The best sources are professionals who've devoted their lives and
careers to trout and water conservation. You'll need biologists, hydrologists and other scientists for technical facts. You'll also
need elected and appointed public officials for their political savvy
and influence. They, in turn, will need you for grass-roots information and support. Who is right shouldn't matter. What is right
should. Instead of dividing and conquering ourselves, put that bur-
den on the opposition.

One of the best ways to get involved and have influence is to join
a trout- or fly-fishing organization. It's neither expensive nor
time-consuming. It is a great way to stay informed, and there's political strength in numbers. A list of Missouri's trout- and fly-
fishing organizations is farther back in the book. If none is near
you, join one of the national organizations also listed there.

TROUT-STALKER CONSERVATION

TROUT STALKERS aren't an endangered species, but we hate to lose them
just the same. You've already learned about safe wading. Here are
some other tips to help you stay alive.

Floods

Missouri trout streams flood. Awesomely. And rapidly. Every year,
a few riverbank campers wake up in the middle of the night with water
surging between their toes and half of their gear headed for New Or-
leans. Others get swept away while driving across the numerous
Ozark road fords and low-water bridges.

If you're wading below Table Rock Dam or Powersite Dam at Lake
Taneycomo, be alert for the man-made floods when the power-generation
turbines start up. Listen for the warning horn, and leave the water
fast when you hear it.

Always keep one eye on the weather forecast, one eye on the sky and
another on the water. Don't be a hero. Drowning takes a lot of the
fun out of fishing.

Heat

One thing Missouri trout waters have never been short of is summer-
time heat. Fish early and late, or wet-wade in Levis and sneakers
through midday. Carry a canteen. Take it slow and easy, especially
to and from the car.

Cold

Every few winters, someone dies from hypothermia on a Missouri
stream. Usually it's a canoer who'se dumped far from help, but it
could happen to wading anglers, too. Winter temperatures can shift
from balmy to bitter in a few short hours, and the amount of river
inside your waders can change in a flash. Dress in layers, carry a
waterproof fire starter, fish with a friend and stay a little closer
to the car.

Drinking Springwater

This one probably won't kill you, but you may think you're going to
die for a while. Even pristine springwater can have lots of micro-
scopic critters able and willing to savage your intestinal tract.
Add to that some barnlot or septic-tank seepage, and you've got a
really potent brew. It'll look, taste and smell perfectly fine, but
it's a time bomb just waiting to explode in your waders.

ANIMAL-RIGHTS ACTIVISTS

I HATE to even mention them, but you may hear or read of 'em sooner
or later. PETA (People for the Ethical Treatment of Animals) is the
most vociferous enemy of sportfishing, but there are other groups,
too.
   The main thing to understand about these folks is that their argu-
ments against us are pure phony baloney, having little or nothing to
do with objective scientific biological reality. Fish in the wild
lead exceedingly high-stress, fright-filled lives just trying to survive, and die quite horrible natural deaths. Anglers, by and large,
are the least of their worries.
   Beginning with the unshakable conviction that they're morally more
righteous than the rest of us, PETA and its sympathizers then conjure
up all kinds of Disney-like fantasyland pseudobiology to justify
their emotional needs. Treat 'em with tolerance, maybe even pity,
don't waste your breath trying to reason with them rationally, and go
right on fishing with a perfectly clear conscience.

HOBBIES AND CRAFTS RELATED TO FLY FISHING

IN ADDITION to fly fishing itself, many folks also enjoy a variety of
related hobbies and crafts. Fly tying probably is the most popular.
You can tie the old standards, improve on them or invent entirely new
patterns.
   Many people enjoy building custom-made rods or crafting landing
nets from fine woods. The best are works of art.
   Photography is another hobby many fly fishers pursue. While you're
at it, surround your photos with a thousand or two artfully crafted
words and send the package to an outdoor magazine. Who knows what
might happen?
   The serious study of aquatic entomology captures some imaginations.
Collect specimens from different streams throughout the year to learn
the insects, their life stages and emergence times. You might even
want to study their life cycles in a home aquarium.
   Fly fishing can involve other sports such as hiking, canoeing and
camping. The fishing's not something to pass the time while doing
these other things—it's the reason for them.
   One hobby that all fly fishers engage in sooner or later is weather
forecasting. "That little cloud over there? Nah. It'll never
amount to anything. C'mon..."

TROUT- AND FLY-FISHING ORGANIZATIONS

THERE ARE a number of trout- and fly-fishing organizations in Missouri. For beginners, they're a great place to learn how to cast, fish, tie flies, build rods and spin tall tales. For everyone, they're a good way to meet new fishing companions, keep up on trout-conservation activities, and help influence the course of Missouri's trout-management and water pollution-control programs.

Because members, officers and meeting places tend to change over the years, none of them has a really permanent address or telephone number. To find them, watch the newspaper for meeting notices, or inquire at tackle shops in the areas where they're located. Also, check out the backs of other anglers' fishing vests. Most organizations have patches their members wear, and that's where you'll see them. Don't be bashful. Most people will be delighted if you ask to join.

Local Organizations

MISSOURI TROUT FISHERMEN'S ASSOCIATION
    There are chapters in Springfield and Kansas City.

ARROWHEAD FLYFISHERS
    Find these folks in east-side Kansas City.

CAPITOL CITY FLY FISHERS
    This bunch hangs out in Jefferson City.

HEART OF AMERICA FLY FISHERS
    This crowd comes from both sides of the state line in Kansas City.

KC NORTHLAND FLY FISHERS
    These folks prowl the north side of Kansas City.

M-A-K-O FLYFISHERS
    This bunch is centered in Joplin.

MISSOURI DEAF FLY FISHERS ASSOCIATION
    These fine folks are from all over. Contact Mike Butler at (573) 634-7955 through the Relay Missouri Center, 1-800-735-2966 for TDD users, or 2466 for the rest of us, if you're interested in hooking up with 'em.

OZARK FLYFISHERS
    This fine group operates in the St. Louis area.

ROUBIDOUX FLY FISHERS
    You'll find these folks in the Waynesville/Ft. Leonard Wood area.

SOUTHWEST MISSOURI FLY FISHERS
    Springfield is where this fine bunch congregates.

TRI-LAKES FLY FISHERS
 Find these fun-lovin' folks in Bolivar.

MID-MISSOURI CHAPTER, TROUT UNLIMITED
 This great bunch is headquartered in Columbia.

SEMO CHAPTER, TROUT UNLIMITED
 These folks get together in Cape Girardeau.

BRANSON CHAPTER, TROUT UNLIMITED
 Shur nuff—Branson is where to find these folks.

State Organizations

CONSERVATION FEDERATION OF MISSOURI
 This outstanding organization is for all Missouri sportsmen, not
 just trout anglers and fly fishers. Contact the Federation at 728
 West Main Street, Jefferson City, Missouri 65101-1559. Their phone
 number is (573)634-2322 or 1-800-575-2322. Their e-mail address is
 mofed@sockets.net.

National Organizations

FEDERATION OF FLY FISHERS (FFF)
 This fine organization is for those who quest for any finny thing
 with the fly rod. All of the local organizations except the three
 Trout Unlimited chapters are affiliated with the FFF. Write to the
 international headquarters at 215 East Lewis Street, Livingston,
 Montana 59047, call there at (406)222-9369, or find 'em on
 the net at fffoffice@fedflyfishers.org.

TROUT UNLIMITED (TU)
 This outstanding group is dedicated to the
 conservation of all coldwater fisheries.
 Contact the national headquarters at
 1300 North 17th Street, Suite 500,
 Arlington, Virginia 22209-3801,
 phone (703)522-0200. On the
 keyboard, find 'em at
 www.tu.org and
 trout@tu.org.

Eagles have to make a living, too.
You'll occasionally see them along
Missouri's larger streams during
the winter.

WHERE THE TROUT ARE

HERE ARE the where-to details I promised you up front. With a map or two under your arm and a few telephone calls, you'll be able to stalk trout anywhere in the state.

Along with all of the other information, I've indicated the U.S. Geological Survey topographic quadrangle map or maps where each location can be found. Order these maps from the Missouri Geological Survey and Resource Assessment Division, PO Box 250, Rolla, Missouri 65402. Give them a call at (573)368-2100. Maps were $6.00 each in 2004.

The trout fishing-regulation information I gave you up front always is subject to change. New regulations usually take effect on March 1 of each year. Copies of the Missouri Wildlife Code are available wherever fishing permits are sold. Waters with special regulations usually have the latest information prominently posted near streamside.

Not all of the resorts, fee-fishing areas, campgrounds and canoe liveries are open year 'round, so it's wise to check ahead, especially from Labor Day through March.

Please understand that the motel, campground, restaurant and canoe-livery listings are not personal recommendations. If you have a bad experience somewhere, chalk it up as an adventure, make up a good story about it, and blame it on them, not me. Thank you.

The Trout Parks

BENNETT SPRING STATE PARK, 26250 Highway 64A, Lebanon, Missouri 65536. For general information, call the park headquarters at (417)532-4338.

Bennett Spring is the oldest and most popular of the four trout parks. Take Highway 64 west from Lebanon twelve miles to get there. You'll find a mile and a half of spring creek 30 to 100 feet wide, full of rainbows and an occasional brown. The upper 2,000 feet of water are reserved for fly fishing only. Except when filled with other anglers and spectators, the backcasting room usually is spacious.

Rental cabins are available in the park. Call (417)532-4307 for reservations between March 1 and October 31. If they're full, there's an abundance of other lodging nearby. On Highway 64A inside the park entrance, stay at Larry's Cedar Resort (417)532-2356. On Highway 64 west of the Niangua River bridge, try the Sand Spring Resort (417)532-5857 or 1-800-543-FISH; or Fort Niangua River Resort (417)532-4377. Between the bridge and Lebanon, try the Circle J Campground (417)532-4430; Vogel's Homestead Resort (417)532-4097 or 1-800-353-4097; Bennett Spring Inn (417)588-9110 or 1-800-IS-TROUT; or the Oakhill Campground (417)532-6447. Lebanon has a dozen more motels.

The park has excellent tent- and RV-camping facilities available on a first-come, first-served basis. On the river's west bank, try the NRO Campground and Canoe Rental (417)532-6333 or 588-3386 or 1-800-748-7249; Maggard's Corkery Campground (417)532-7616; or One-Eyed Willy's Campground. On the east bank, stay at Redbeard's Ranch (weekends only) (417)533-REDS; or Ho-Humm Canoe Rental and Campground (417)588-1908. Elsewhere, try the Fort Bennett Tradin' Post (417)588-

1391; Vogel's Homestead Resort (417)532-4097 or 1-800-353-4097; Circle J Campground (417)532-4430; Fort Niangua River Resort (417)532-4377; Idle Time RV Park & Campground (417)588-1631; Menagerie Campground (417)532-3724; Adventures Campground (417)588-RAFT; R & W Canoe Rental (417)588-3358 or 1-800-969-0552; Riverfront Campground & Canoe Rental (417)588-3386 or 1-888-67-FRONT; Cedar Ridge Campground (417)532-9622; or the Oakhill Campground (417)532-6447.

There's an excellent restaurant in the park, and the Hillbilly Burger is on Highway 64A inside the park. Across the river, dine at the Sand Spring Resort. East of the river along Highway 64, find a meal at the Circle J Cafe or Thompson's Creel Store & RV Park.

Be sure to check out the Spring View Fly Shop and Motel (417)588-2116 and Reading's Fly Shop (417)588-4334, both on Highway 64 a short distance east of the park entrance. Gaston's Tackle & Gift Shop (417) 532-9449 and Larry's Sporting Goods (417)532-8678 also carry good selections of fly-fishing necessities.

You'll find Bennett Spring State Park on the Bennett Spring 7.5-minute quadrangle map.

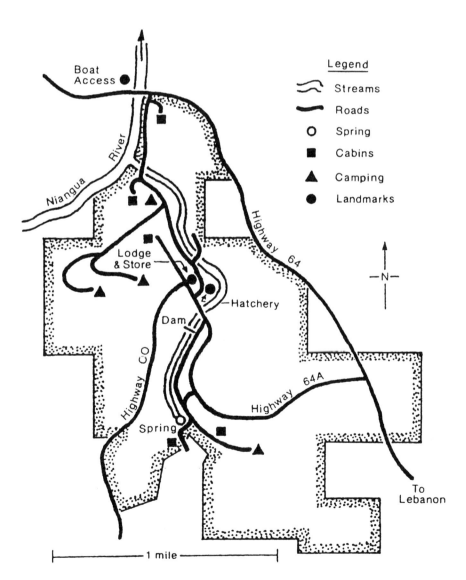

MARAMEC SPRING PARK, 21880 Maramec Spring Drive, St. James, Missouri 65559. The phone number is (573)265-7124 or 7387.
   To reach this popular spot, take Highway 8 east for seven miles from St. James or west ten miles from Steelville. Fishing is for mostly rainbows in one mile of large spring creek. Unlike the other trout parks, this one has no flies-only water.

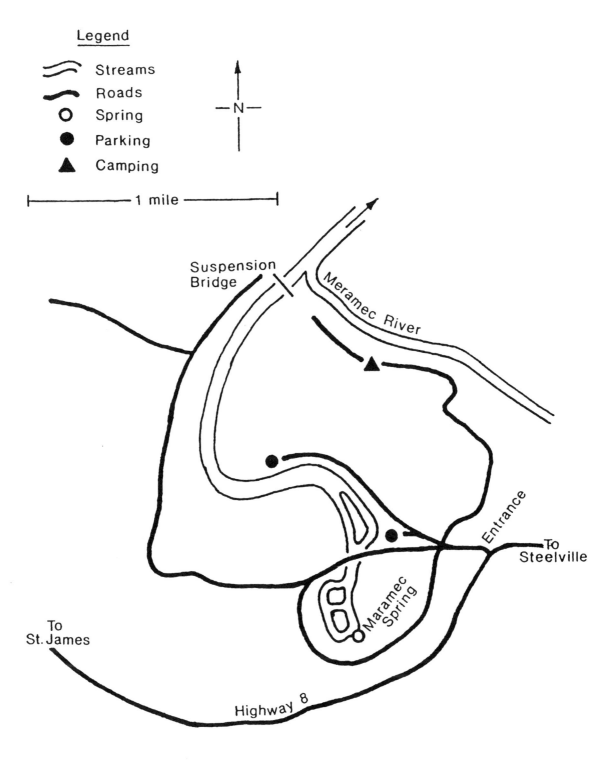

The park offers much in addition to trout fishing. There's a reception center, restaurant, nature center, museum, historic iron works, playground, courts, picnic tables, trout-rearing pools, observation towers and a full-facility campground.

Cabins are available at Buck's Lodge on Highway 8 1-3/4 miles west of the park (573)265-7922; Lost Creek Ranch ¼ mile west (573)368-6878 or 265-7407; and at Green's Canoe Rental & Campground 3½ miles east (573)775-5595 or 1-800-815-6721. Elsewhere, stay in St. James at the Economy Inn (573)265-3256; Comfort Inn (573)265-5005; Finn's Motel (573)265-7200; or the Painted Lady Bed & Breakfast (573)265-5008. In Steelville, try the Meramec Inn (573)775-5800; Wildwood Springs Resort (573)775-2400; Frisco Street Bed & Breakfast (573)775-4247; or Parkview Farm Bed & Breakfast (573)775-4195. The Indian Springs Resort four miles west of Steelville off Highway 8 also has lodging. Call (573)775-2266 or 1-800-392-1110.

If the park campground is full, try the Meramec Springs Country Store on Highway 8, 1½ miles west of the park (573)265-3796. If that's full, too, try the Pheasant Acres Campground ¼ mile farther west (573)265-5149; the nearby Old Iron Town Park (573)265-1223; Green's Canoe Rental & Campground; the Indian Springs Resort; or the Candy Cane RV Park & Campground west of Steelville (573)775-2889.

During the summer, you can eat at the park or Indian Springs Resort. Otherwise, St. James has seven places to dine, and Steelville has six.

Maramec Spring Park is located on the Maramec Spring 7.5-minute quadrangle map.

MONTAUK STATE PARK, Route 5, Box 279, Salem, Missouri 65560. For general information, phone (573)548-2201. For camping, cabin and motel reservations, phone (573)548-2434.

Montauk is located at the southern terminus of Highway 119 in Dent County. It offers rainbow trout fishing, and an occasional brown, in 2½ miles of the upper Current River. The water's twenty to fifty feet wide, and the backcasting room varies from fair to fantastic. There are two areas reserved for fly fishing only, one of which is catch-and-release only.

Park facilities include a lodge, store, restaurant, trout hatchery, motel, cabins, campground, picnic areas, grist mill, conference center and hiking trails.

The park's motel and cabins are heavily booked, especially during the summer. The nearest other lodging is Reed's Cabins at the park entrance. Call there at (573)548-2222. Cahill Country Store and Cabins is only a quarter mile more distant. Call it at (573)548-0106. Otherwise, stay in Licking at the Country Inn Motel (573)674-3466 or 2114, or the Best Value Inn (573)674-4809. In Salem, overnight at the Holiday Inn Express (573)729-4700, Walnut Motel (573)729-3121, Crossroads Inn (573)729-4191 or 1-877-912-2054, or Ranch Motel (573)729-3157.

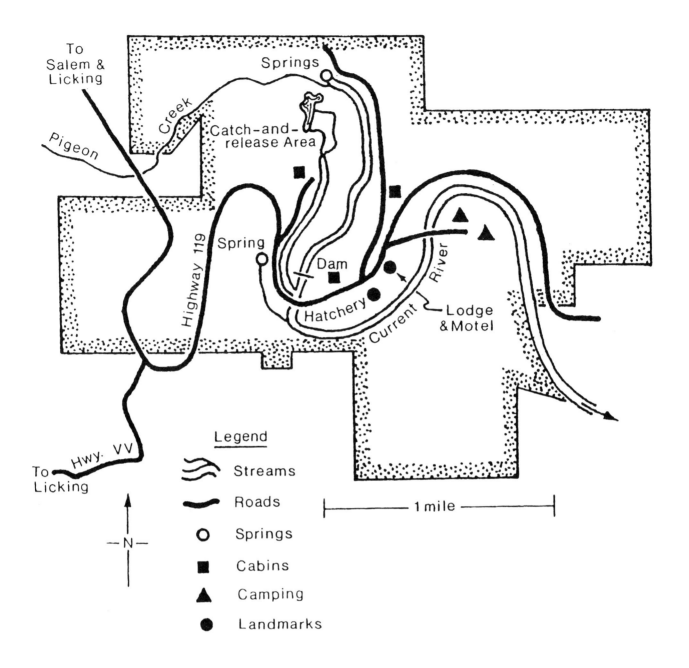

To
Salem &
Licking

Springs

Creek

Pigeon

Catch-and-
release Area

Highway 119

Spring

Dam

Hatchery

Current River

Lodge
& Motel

To
Licking

Hwy. VV

Legend

Streams

Roads

○ Springs

■ Cabins

▲ Camping

● Landmarks

⊢——— 1 mile ———⊣

—N—

The large park campground has complete tent- and RV-camping facilities, but it's often full. The Ozark Mountain Ranch Campground is
only 1½ miles east. You also can stay at the Pine Crest Campground
on Highway YY east of the park (573)548-3344. Campers can find groceries at the park lodge, Reed's Cabins and the Cahill Country Store.

If you pass up the park restaurant, dine at nine places in Licking
or a baker's dozen in Salem.

You'll find Montauk State Park on the Montauk 7.5-minute quadrangle map.

ROARING RIVER STATE PARK, Route 4, Box 4100, Cassville, Missouri 65625. For general information, call (417)847-2539. For cabin and motel reservations, call (417)847-2330.
 Cold, clear water pouring from Roaring River Cave provides superb

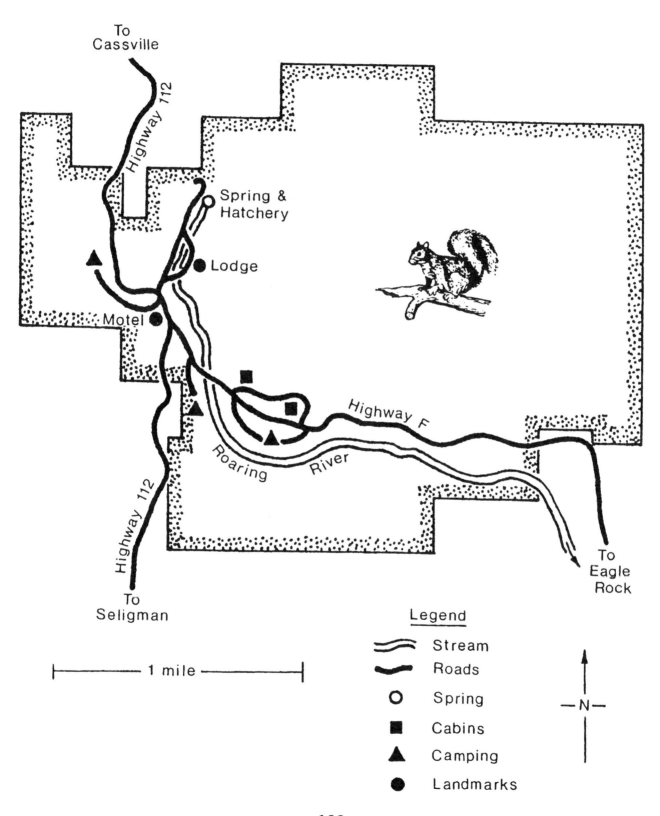

To Cassville

Highway 112

Spring & Hatchery

Lodge

Motel

Cabins

Highway F

Roaring River

Highway 112

To Seligman

To Eagle Rock

1 mile

Legend

~~~ Stream
~ Roads
○ Spring
■ Cabins
▲ Camping
● Landmarks

—N—

rainbow trout fishing in 2½ miles of beautiful water below. There's a special section for fly fishing only, and a catch-and-release section featuring more than a few lunker brown trout with some swimmers and waders mixed in. And, Roaring River, both in the park and below, offers your only hope of catching a brook trout in Missouri. Every now and then, a few swim up here from the Beaver Lake tailwaters in Arkansas.

The park has just about every feature you could desire—spectacular scenery, a trout hatchery, nature center, swimming pool, restaurant, hiking trails, tent camping and RV hookups, cabins and a motel.

If the park lodging is full, there are many other possibilities nearby. In Cassville, stay at the Super 8 Motel (417)847-4888; Cassville Motor Inn (417)847-6235; Budget Inn Motel (417)847-4196; or Rainbow Motel (417)847-2234.

Between Cassville and the park on Highway 112, try the Sportsman's Lodge (417)847-2030; Fisherman's Inn (417)847-3398; Oakhill Court (417)847-2988; Rock Village Court (417)847-2323; Sunset Motel (417) 847-2903; or the Seven Valleys Motel (417)847-2161.

If you'd rather camp outside the park, try the Roaring River Resort RV Park & Campground (417)847-3235; or the Rock Village Court.

You can dine at the park restaurant or sixteen places in Cassville. Between the two, try the Hilltop Restaurant, Rex's Family Restaurant or Beebe's Roaring River Cafe.

There are two local fly-fishing shops to serve your needs. Tim's Fly Shop is on Highway 112 north of the park next to the Sportsmen's Lodge. Call Tim at (417)847-4956, or e-mail him at timsfly@hotmail. com. There's also a well-stocked shop in the park lodge.

You'll find Roaring River State Park on the Eagle Rock 7.5-minute quadrangle map.

Blue Ribbon Waters

BARREN FORK, Shannon County.

Ya cain't hardly git here from where you are, but it's a lotta _fun_ if ya do.

This is a wonderful little stream ten to twenty feet wide with a modest population of brightly colored, streambred rainbows in a beautiful landscape. It isn't near anywhere, and the amount of public access is limited. The privately owned parts are zealously protected against trespass.

To find the upper half mile below Twin Springs, take Highway A west for thirteen miles from Bunker, or east for 2-3/4 miles from the defunct community of Timber (the entering and leaving signs are on opposite sides of the same post) on Highway 19. Turn south onto Shannon County Road AD at the Chrisco Cemetery sign, and park at the low-water crossing over the creek. Wade downstream for several hundred feet to the mouth of Twin Springs Branch to begin fishing.

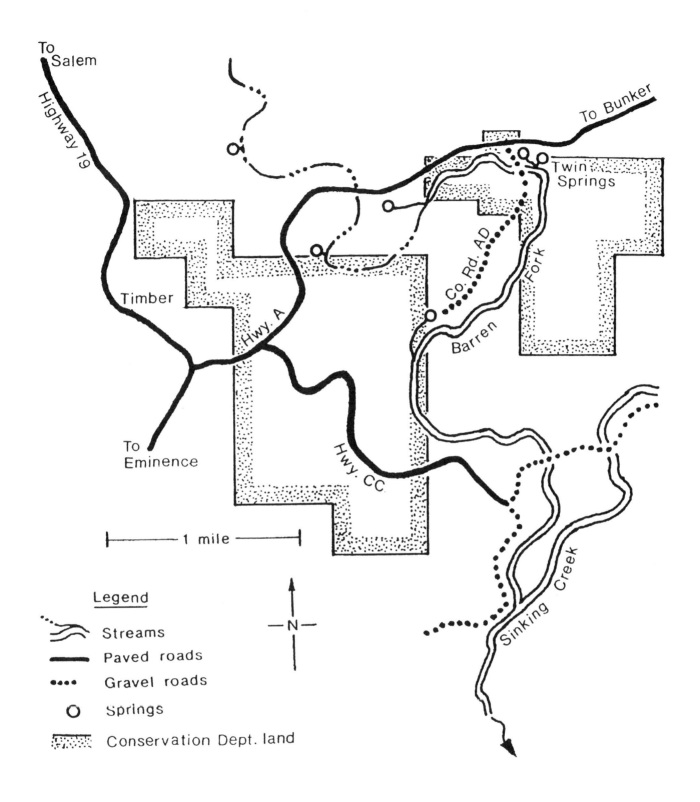

To Salem

Highway 19

To Bunker

Twin
Springs

Timber

Hwy. A

Co. Rd. AD

Fork

Barren

To
Eminence

Hwy. CC

Sinking Creek

⊢———— 1 mile ————⊣

Legend

·∿∿∿ Streams

——— Paved roads

•••• Gravel roads

O Springs

Conservation Dept. land

—N—

    Access to the lower half mile on down the valley is by an obscure
woods road off Highway A, then turning right along the property-line
fence until it reaches the creek. A copy of the Round Spring quadrangle map will help keep you from straying off the Conservation Department land.

The nearest motels are in Salem and Eminence. Closer to the water, rent a cabin at Jason Place Campground (573)858-3228 or 1-800-365-2537, and at Larimore's Hard Rock Campground & General Store (573) 858-3345 or 1-800-297-3345, both five miles north from Timber on Highway 19, then three miles west on Highway KK. The Round Spring Lodge at Timber is sometimes open, usually not. Inquire about it at Jason Place.

Other camping possibilities incluyde the Running River Canoe Rental one-half mile south of the Highway A turnoff (573)858-3371 or 1-800-226-6394; and the National Park Service's Current River campgrounds at Pulltite Spring on Highway EE off Highway 19 south of Timber, and at Round Spring on Highway 19 seven miles south of Timber. Call (573) 323-4236 for information on both. For really primitive camping, try the Land of Zoe Campground five miles south on Highway 19.

The nearest restaurants are at Jason Place and Larimore's. Otherwise, it's 19 miles south of Timber to Eminence or 24 miles north to Salem. Bunker sometimes has a restaurant, sometimes not.

Find this little trout-fishing delight on the Round Spring and Gladden 7.5-minute quadrangle maps.

BLUE SPRING CREEK, Crawford County.

To get here, leave Interstate 44 at exit 218 at Bourbon, and go five miles south on Highway N.

This is an enchanting little stream with wildbred rainbow trout up to a couple pounds, rarely even larger. It's only five to twenty feet wide, and the backcasting room can be a little scarce at times. Below the Salvation Army's Camp Mihaska, the trout-holding portion of the creek is state-owned all the way to its mouth.

The Blue Springs Ranch Campground and Canoe Rental on the Thickety Ford Road at the creek's mouth offers both camping and rental cabins. Call there at (573) 732-5200 or 1-800-333-8007. You can also camp or rent a cabin at the Riverview Ranch at Campbell Bridge over the Meramec River on Highway N, four miles south of the Thickety Ford Road intersection. Call there at (573)732-5544 or 1-800-RIV-VIEW. In Bourbon, stay at the Budget Inn Motel (573)732-4080. Dine in Bourbon at the Hen House Restaurant, Scoops 'n'

Blue Spring Creek

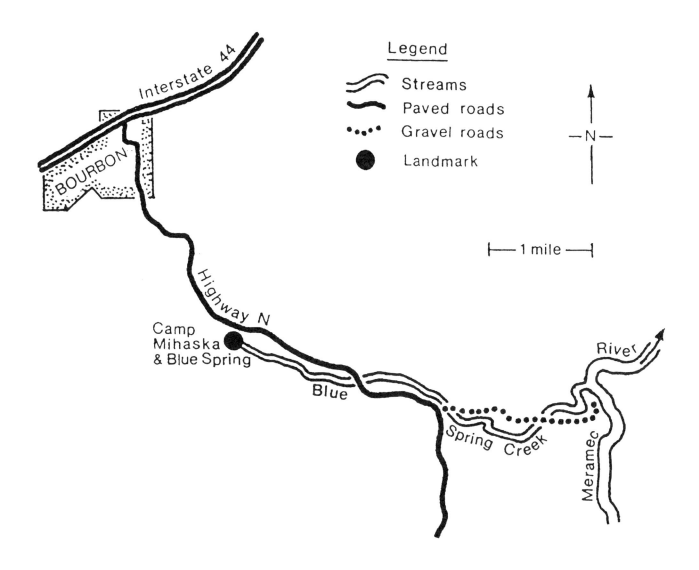

CRANE CREEK, Stone County.
   This is a captivating little stream five to twenty-five feet wide which flows through the town of Crane. Streambred rainbows are found from the spring source all the way down to a mile below the mouth of Spring Creek.
   Public access is in the Crane City Park and on two stretches owned by the Conservation Department. The longest stretch is on the Wire Road Wildlife Area from the west edge of town upstream for two miles to the second low-water bridge. The other provides access to half a mile of the creek downstream from the first bridge below town at Quail Spur Crossing. Don't overlook the city-park water just because it's in the center of town.

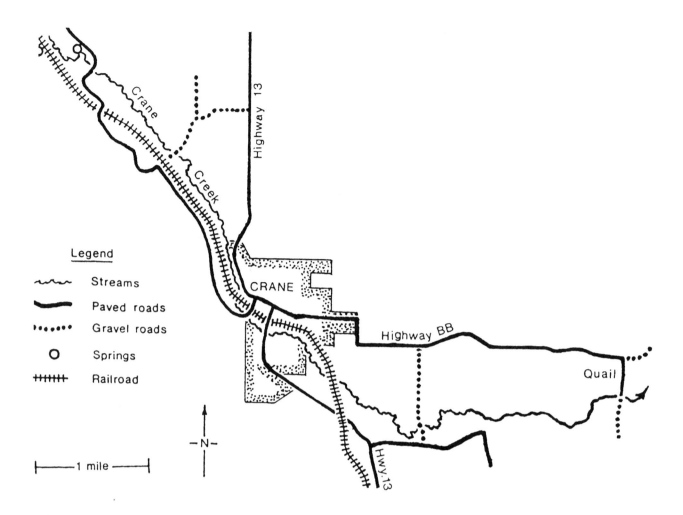

Legend

~~~~ Streams

‾‾‾ Paved roads

••••• Gravel roads

O Springs

++++++ Railroad

├── 1 mile ──┤

—N—

Crane Creek has long been thought to be one of only four known places on the face of our planet where the genetically pure strain of McCloud River rainbow trout still survives, but that belief has been questioned in recent years. Dna studies so far are inconclusive, so stay tuned.

The nearest lodging is in Aurora at the Aurora Inn Motel (417)678-5035 and the Bluebird Motel (417)678-5757.

The nearest camping is at the Corps of Engineers' large recreation area at Cape Fair. Facilities include everything the tent or RV camper might desire.

You can dine in Crane at the Crane Creek Family Restaurant, Crane Cafe, Gary & Jan's Dairy Lane or Chuck's Waffle House. Aurora has twenty-two places to eat, and Marionville has half a dozen.

You'll find this trout-fishing delight on the Crane 7.5-minute quadrangle map.

CURRENT RIVER, Dent County.
This water begins at the lower boundary of Montauk State Park and extends eight miles downstream to the Cedargrove Access. It's administered by the National Park Service as part of the Ozark National Scenic Riverways.

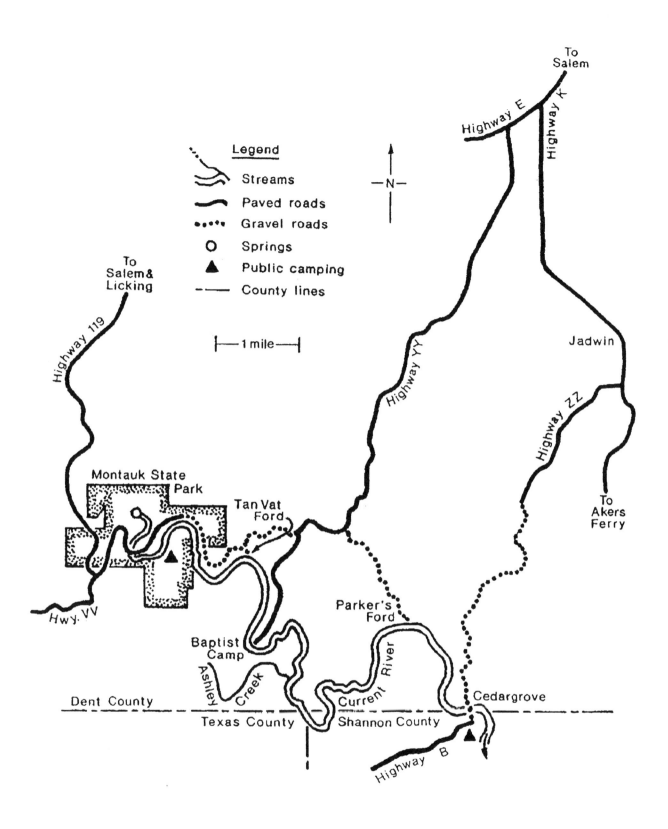

A wild and beautiful stream enclosed by picturesque dolostone bluffs, it offers fine angling for a few rainbows and many browns, some of which reach sixteen pounds. The water's 30 to 100 feet wide, and wadable in all but a few places. The backcasting room's occasionally tight, but it's mostly fair to great.

The daily limit is one fish of eighteen inches or more in length. Natural baits are forbidden here.

Vehicular access is at Montauk State Park, Tan Vat Ford, Baptist Camp Access, Parker's Ford and Cedargrove. Get to Montauk on Highway 119. Follow your nose onto the gravel (Dent County Road 667) at the blacktop's end. Tan Vat is about one mile beyond; the turnoff to Baptist Camp is about a mile beyond Tan Vat; and the turnoff to Parker's Ford (Dent County Road 652) is another two-thirds of a mile beyond that. To reach Cedargrove, turn off Highway K south of Salem onto Highway ZZ and follow your nose for a little more than five miles, or take Highway B east from Houston or Raymondville.

Check the section on Montauk State Park for lodging, camping and dining information there and in Licking and Salem. Refer there, too, for camping facilities near the water's upper end.

Near the lower end, rent a mobile home at Barton's Lodging (573)729-5197 or camp at Big Rock Candy Mountain Cabins, Camping, Bar and Grill on Highway B one mile west of Cedargrove (417)932-6917; Whispering Pines Trail Ride two miles north of Cedargrove (573)729-7591; Jadwin Canoe Rental at Jadwin (573)729-5229 or 1-800-937-4837; or the Park Service's primitive campground at Cedargrove. The Jadwin Canoe Rental and Paul's Store across the road both have groceries. Dine at Big Rock Candy Mountain, or at Acleda's Korner Kitchen in Raymondville.

Rent canoes at the Jadwin Canoe Rental. Reserve your canoe well in advance during the summer.

The blue-ribbon portion of the Current River flows across the Montauk and Cedargrove 7.5-minute quadrangle maps.

Current River country

ELEVEN POINT RIVER, Oregon County.

The Eleven Point is a segment of the nation's National Scenic River System. It's administered by the U.S. Forest Service as part of the Mark Twain National Forest.

From 50 to 150 feet wide, it holds rainbows up to ten pounds. The blue-ribbon water begins at the mouth of Greer Spring and extends six miles downstream to the Turner Mill Access. Bait is not allowed, and you can keep one fish per day, eighteen inches or larger. Vehicular access is at the Highway 19 bridge and Turner Mill.

Nearby lodging includes the Motel 60 (573)325-4416 or 4727 and the Rusty Nail Motel (573)325-4223, both in Winona, and the Alton Motel in Alton (417)778-6208. At Greer, Richards' Canoe Rental and Campground offers cabins and sleeping rooms (417)778-6186.

Campers can stay at the Forest Service's Greer Crossing Campground on the river at Highway 19, or at McCormack Lake a few miles north.

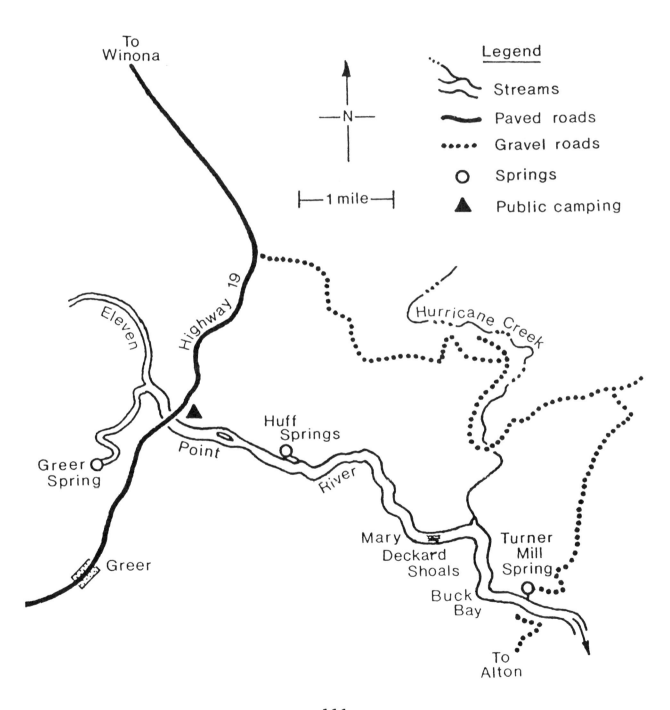

Both offer pads, tables, grills, drinking water and toilets. Richards' Canoe Rental and Campground at Greer offers complete tent and RV camping.

Dine in Winona at Linda's Cafe or Flossie's Apple Barrel, or in Alton at Benita's Cafe, Thompson's Restaurant, Taylor's Pizza or Grandma's Kitchen.

Much of this water is deep and accessible only by canoe. Rent one from Richards' Canoe Rental and Campground, or from the Eleven Point Canoe Rental at Alton (417)778-6497. Be careful running Mary Deckard Shoals—it's a canoe killer.

The blue-ribbon portion of the Eleven Point River is on the Greer, Many Springs and Wilderness 7.5-minute quadrangle maps.

Mary Deckard Shoals on the Eleven Point

LITTLE PINEY CREEK, Phelps County.

The blue-ribbon section of Little Piney Creek extends from the Dent/Phelps County line ten miles downstream to the Milldam Hollow Access. The first mile and a half, however, only flow intermittently.

Although a few stockers from the white-ribbon water below undoubtedly find their way up here, most of these rainbows are wild, stream-

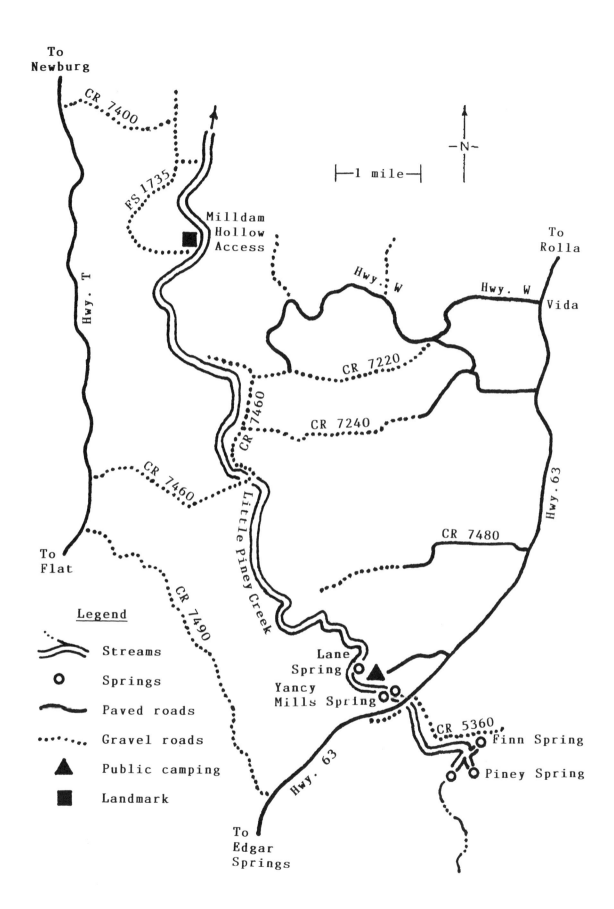

To
Newburg

CR 7400

FS 1735

Milldam
Hollow
Access

Hwy. T

─N─

⊢── 1 mile ──⊣

To
Rolla

Hwy. W

Hwy. W

Vida

CR 7220

CR 7460

CR 7240

CR 7460

Hwy. 63

CR 7480

To
Flat

CR 7490

Little Piney Creek

Legend

Streams

Springs

Paved roads

Gravel roads

Public camping

Landmark

Lane
Spring

Yancy
Mills Spring

CR 5360

Finn Spring

Piney Spring

Hwy. 63

To
Edgar
Springs

bred fish. The highest numbers are upstream. The population thins out as you progress downstream, but that's where some of the largest fish historically have been. Your daily limit here is one 18-incher, and bait is not allowed.

Significant stretches of National Forest water are located above and below the Milldam Hollow Access, and at the Lane Spring Recreation Area. The former is accessible year 'round, the latter is gated shut during the winter. Call the Forest Service at (417)967-4194 for current opening and closing dates. When closed, the water can be reached less conveniently from beneath the Highway 63 bridge. This is private land. Keep it clean or lose it!

Lodging most convenient to the lower end of this water is at the western edge of Rolla. Check the Mill Creek writeup for information there. The Rustic Motel on Highway 63 at the southern edge of Rolla is most convenient to the upper end. Call (573)364-6943.

The Lane Spring Recreation Area offers a pavilion, picnic tables, grills, drinking water, camping pads and privies. The 3 Springs RV Campground is at the junction of Highways 63 and M north of Edgar Springs.

Rolla overflows with places to satisfy your hunger. In Edgar Springs, do it at the Town Cafe.

Find this wonderful water on the Yancy Mills and Kaintuck Hollow quadrangle maps.

MILL CREEK, Phelps County.

This is a beautiful little stream five to twenty feet wide with brightly colored streambred rainbows up to several pounds. It's tightly enclosed in fly-eating brush and trees for much of its publicly accessible length.

Get here by taking Interstate 44 exit 179 and following Highway T south through Newburg. Cross Little Piney Creek and immediately turn right onto Highway P. Follow it for three miles, turn left onto County Road 7550, and follow this for two miles to the Forest Service's Mill Creek Recreation Area.

There's public water from the recreation area downstream for $1\frac{1}{2}$ miles and upstream for about two-thirds of a mile, but it's private water for the next $1\frac{1}{4}$ mile above that. Then comes another two miles of public water. Don't bother fishing in Wilkins Spring Branch. The Forest Service eradicated all the trout in there long ago.

Fishing is an on-again, off-again proposition above the low-water crossing between Highway AA and Wilkins Spring. In years when high water completely submerges the crossing, numbers of trout migrate into the creek above it as far as Yelton Spring, and remain there when the creek recedes. The fishing can be excellent in this section until it dries up, which it does in about half of all summers.

The nearest motels are at Interstate 44 exit 184 on the western edge of Rolla. Call the Super 8 Motel (573)364-4156; Days Inn (573) 341-3700; Best Value Inn & Suites 1-888-315-BEST; Best Western Coachlight Inn (573)341-2511; Econo Lodge (573)341-3130; Holiday Inn Express (573)364-8200; Western Inn (573)341-3050; Zeno's Motel & Steak

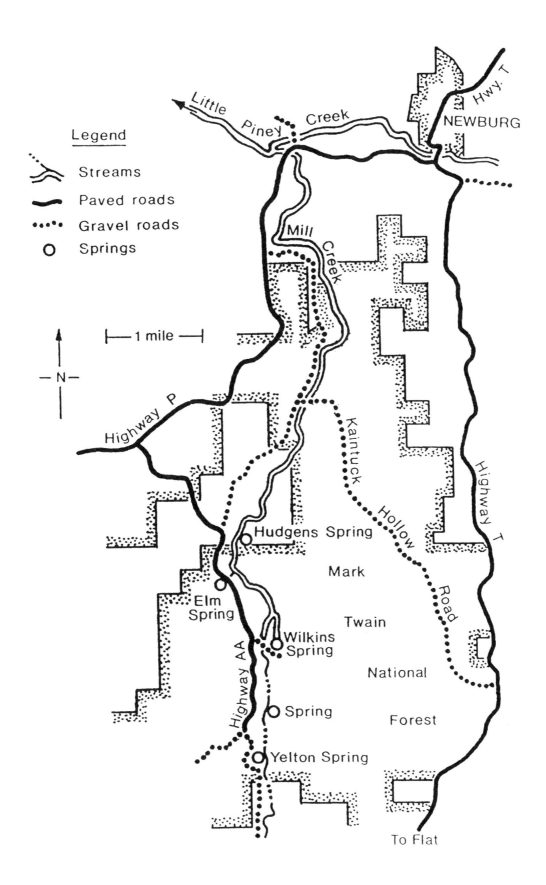

Legend

〜 Streams

— Paved roads

•••• Gravel roads

O Springs

1 mile

—N—

Little Piney Creek

NEWBURG

Hwy. T

Mill Creek

Highway P

Kaintuck Hollow

Hudgens Spring

Mark

Elm Spring

Twain

Wilkins Spring

Highway AA

Highway T

Road

Spring

National

Yelton Spring

Forest

To Flat

—115—

House (573)364-1301; Bestway Inn (573)341-2158; or AmeriHost Inn & Suites (573)364-7000 or 1-800-434-5800.

Restaurants come and go in Newburg. Your best bet for a good meal nearby is PD's Cookin' From Scratch at the BP service station at Interstate 44 exit 179 in Doolittle. Rolla has too many restaurants to list.

You'll find Mill Creek on the Kaintuck Hollow and Newburg 7.5-minute quadrangle maps.

NORTH FORK OF THE WHITE RIVER, Ozark County.

Blue-ribbon regulations begin at the upper outlet of Rainbow (Double) Spring, and extend downstream for almost eight miles to Patrick Bridge. Most of the fish are streambred rainbows, but a few brown trout wander up here from below, too. The browns go up to fourteen pounds, the rainbows up to six or more.

Terminal tackle is limited to artificials only, except that soft plastic baits are off limits. The creel limit is one per day, 18 inches or larger.

It's a big, turbulent river, 40 to 120 feet wide with heavy, boulder-strewn riffles separated by long slicks and deep pools. Much of the bottom is slippery bedrock, so be sure to have felted or cleated waders on. Even with them, you still must wade carefully.

Public access is limited to Kelly Ford, the Conservation Department's access below Blair Bridge, and Patrick Bridge. Overnighting at the River of Life Farm, however, can gain you choice access at The Falls, and camping at Pettit's Canoe Rental can gain you access around Blair Bridge. You'll need a canoe or raft to reach the rest of the water, and the traffic gets pretty heavy during the summer, especially on the weekends. If you're part of it, be careful shooting The Falls. Submerged stuff you can't see makes it worse than it looks.

Nearby lodging is abundant. The River of Life Farm is in the heart of the area. Call there at (417)261-7777 or find 'em on the web at www.riveroflifefarm.com. Also rent the Ozark County Anglers Cabin just below Kelly Ford (417)261-2297 or (816)765-5126. Only a little more distant, rent a cabin or room at Taylormade River Treks near James Bridge (417)284-3055; Dawt Mill (417)284-3540; Riverside Canoe Rental below Patrick Bridge (417)284-3043; North Fork Outfitters at Dora (417)261-2259; Dream-N-Drive RV Park & Motel at Tecumseh (417) 284-1510 or 1-888-865-5776; or Dreamscape Cottages & Campground on Highway 160 west of Tecumseh (417)679-2672 or 1-877-4-U-DREAM.

Farther away, stay in Gainesville at the Antler Motel (417)679-4598 or 4253; or Vaught's Restaurant & Motel (417)679-1080. West Plains has seven motels. The Ramada Inn (417)256-8191 is most convenient to the river.

Camping opportunities are abundant, too. Try the Sunburst Ranch above Patrick Bridge (417)284-3443; Pettit's Canoe Rental at Blair Bridge (417)284-3290; Riverside Canoe Rental below Patrick Bridge (417)284-3043; North Fork Campground at Dora (417)256-1162; Dreamscape Cottages and Campground; the Conservation Department's campground at Patrick Bridge (no drinking water); the Corps of Engineers' Public Use

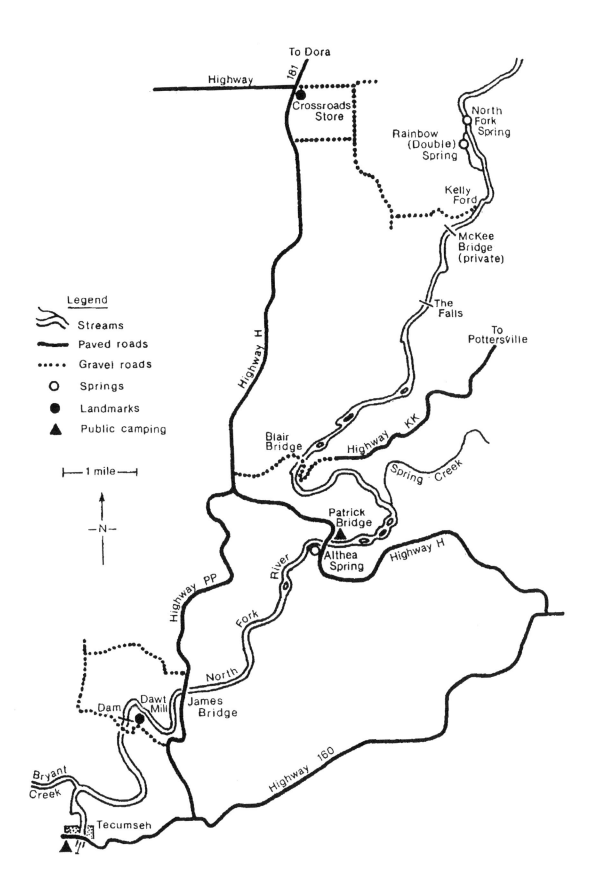

Legend

Streams

Paved roads

Gravel roads

O Springs

● Landmarks

▲ Public camping

⊢— 1 mile —⊣

—N→

To Dora

Highway

181

Crossroads
Store

North
Fork
Spring

Rainbow
(Double)
Spring

Kelly
Ford

McKee
Bridge
(private)

The
Falls

To
Pottersville

Highway H

Blair
Bridge

Highway KK

Spring Creek

Patrick
Bridge ▲

Althea
Spring

Highway H

Highway PP

North Fork River

Dam

Dawt
Mill

James
Bridge

Highway 160

Bryant
Creek

Tecumseh

▲

Area at Tecumseh; or the Classic RV Park east of Hardenville (417)679-2328.

Several of the lodging and camping places nearest the river offer dining or catered meals by prior arrangement. Inquire when you call for reservations. You can also find sit-down meals at the Crossroads Cafe and Grocery south of Dora; Roy's Store at Dora; and the Cruisin' USA Cafe at Tecumseh. Gainesville has five places to eat, and West Plains has many.

Canoes, inflatable rafts and car-shuttle service are available at Riverside Canoe Rental (417)284-3043; North Fork Outfitters (417)261-2259; Dawt Mill (417)284-3540; Pettit's Canoe Rental (417)284-3290; Sunburst Ranch (417)284-3443; River of Life Farm (417)261-7777; and Ozark County Canoe & Kayak (417)261-2331.

The North Fork is Missouri's only trout river where skilled fly-fishing guides and instruction are available. Call Taylormade River Treks (417)284-3055; Dennis Galyardt (417)284-3320; or Myron McKee at River of Life Farm (417)261-7777.

You'll find the blue-ribbon section of the North Fork River on the Cureall NW 7.5-minute quadrangle map.

SPRING CREEK, Phelps County.
This is a pleasant stream twenty to forty feet wide near the east entrance to Ft. Leonard Wood. Badly ravaged by cattle and gravel dredgers in the past, it is mending slowly. It'll be a lot better thirty years from now.

Public access is limited to the lower three miles which are part of the Mark Twain National Forest. The privately owned water above is zealously protected, but it's the breeding ground that provides many of the rainbows downstream.

To get here, leave Interstate 44 at exit 169 and take Highway J south for about eight miles. Just beyond the junction of Highways J and M, you can turn left onto a rough gravel road before the Spring

Relfe (Coppedge) Spring

Creek bridge and follow it upstream for about one-half mile. Or, you can turn left onto County Road 6410 beyond the bridge and follow it all the way up the Spring Creek valley. Relfe (Coppedge) Spring is the upper limit of the trout-holding water.

The nearest lodging is at Interstate 44 exit 163. Stay there at the Best Western Montis Inn (573)336-4299 or 1-800-528-1234; Days Inn (573)336-5556 or 1-800-DAYS-INN; or the Villager Lodge (573)336-3036. The Villager Lodge also has full RV facilities. Near Edgar Springs, stay at the 3 Springs RV Campground near the Highway 63 and Highway M intersection north of town.

Near Interstate 44 exit 163, dine at the Kountry Kookin Family Restaurant, Subway, Country Cafe or Sweetwater Bar-B-Que. In Edgar Springs, fill up at the Town Cafe.

You'll find the trout-holding portion of Spring Creek on the Big Piney, Devils Elbow and Flat 7.5-minute quadrangle maps.

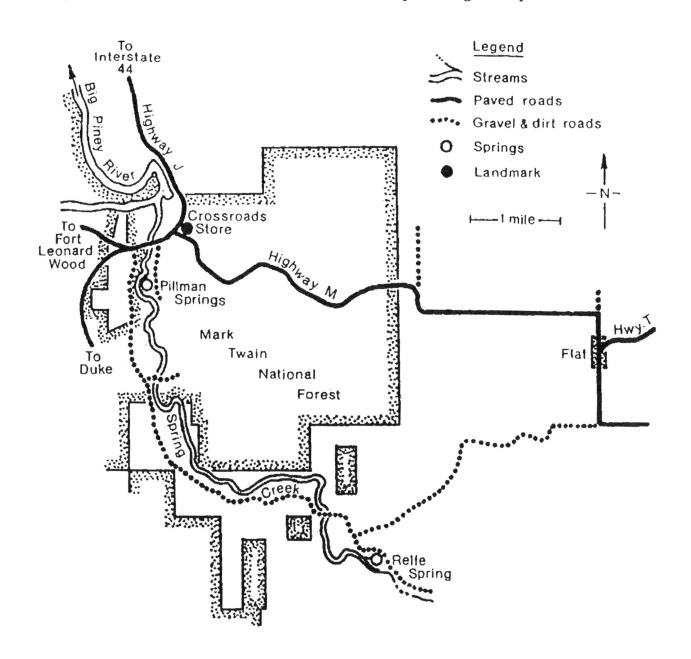

Red Ribbon Waters

MERAMEC RIVER, Phelps and Crawford Counties.
This superb stretch of trout water begins at the Highway 8 bridge one mile east of Maramec Spring Park and extends nine miles down-

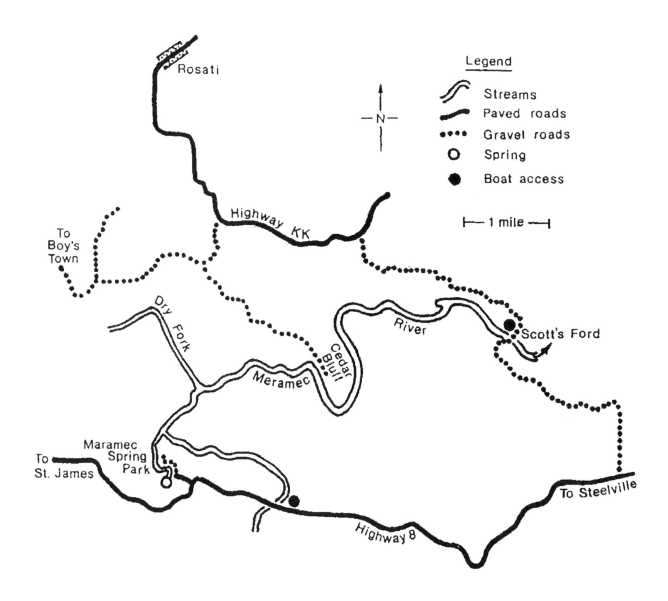

stream to Scott's Ford. It's beautiful water 40 to 100 feet wide with brown and rainbow trout up to eight pounds or more. There's spacious backcasting room, but your fly is just as likely to land in a canoe as on the water during much of the summer. If you can surmount that obstacle, the creel limit is two per day, fifteen inches or better. Natural baits are not allowed.

The upper two miles from Highway 8 to the mouth of Maramec Spring are seldom worth much attention because of the warm summer water. The four miles below Maramec Spring are easily accessible to walking and wading anglers. The lower three miles are best reached by canoe. Discourteous jet boaters are an occasional, but real, hazard everywhere.

Public access is at Highway 8, Maramec Spring Park, Scott's Ford, and the Cardiac Hill and Suicide Hill walk-ins (climb-downs) off the road to Cedar Bluff.

Lodging, camping and dining information is in the section about Maramec Spring Park.

For a canoe, call the Meramec Springs Country Store (573)265-3796; Green's Canoe Rental & Campground (573)775-5595; Buck's Lodge & Canoe Rental (573)265-7922; or Adventure Outdoors (573)775-5744 or 1-800-324-2674. The latter also has rafts and jonboats.

This portion of the Meramec River is located on the Maramec Spring and Indian Springs 7.5-minute quadrangle maps.

The pilings above the mouth of Dry Fork.

NORTH FORK OF THE WHITE RIVER, Ozark County.

Downstream from the blue-ribbon water, six miles of the North Fork from Patrick Bridge to Norfork Lake are managed under regulations allowing you to creel two fish per day, 15 inches or larger, and any kind of terminal tackle is okay. This is primarily brown trout water, but there are a lot of streambred rainbows, too.

Public access is at Patrick Bridge and James Bridge. Privately owned access available to the public is at Riverside Canoe Rental below Patrick Bridge and Dawt Mill.

Refer to the section on the North Fork's blue-ribbon section for a map and detailed information on lodging, camping, dining, canoe and guide services.

ROUBIDOUX CREEK, Pulaski County.

Fed by the surging waters of Roubidoux Spring, Roubidoux Creek flows through the City of Waynesville to the Gasconade River three miles away. In contrast to the almost-anything-goes regulations upstream, the lower $2\frac{1}{4}$ miles below the overhead utility line crossing the creek near the downstream end of the city park are managed under special regulations for quality sportfishing.

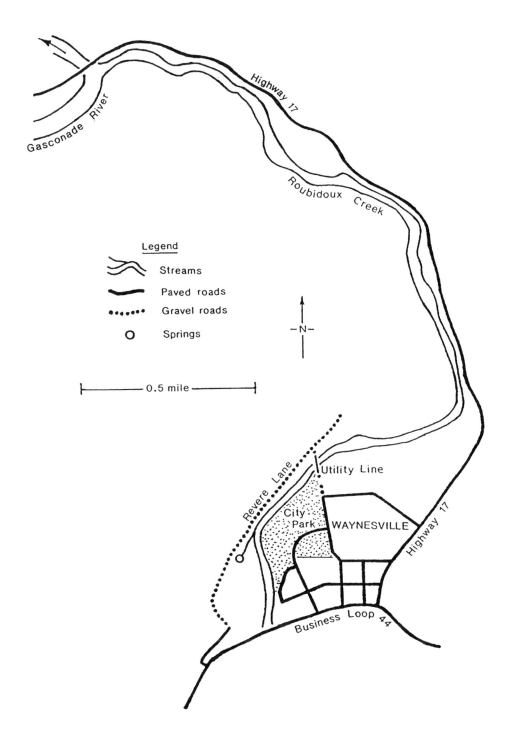

Full of scrappy brown trout and more than a few rainbows, this section is easily accessible by road almost everywhere. The water's twenty to fifty feet wide, and the backcasting's usually easy. Terminal tackle is restricted to flies and artificial lures, and only two fish at least fifteen inches long may be creeled daily. For best luck here, confine your fishing during the worst heat of summer to the morning hours and ignore the mile of water above the creek's mouth.

The nearest lodging is in St. Robert. The Star Motel (573)336-3223 or 1-800-953-2506 is nearest the water. Other places include the Holiday Inn Express (573)336-2299; Motel 6 (573)336-3610; Econo Lodge (573)336-7272; Budget Inn (573)336-5212 or 1-800-308-3309; Ramada Inn (573)336-3121; Red Roof Inn (573)336-2510 or 1-800-RED-ROOF; Baymont Inn & Suites (573)336-5050; Candlewood Suites (573)451-2500; Fairfield Inn (573)336-8600; Comfort Inn (573)336-3553; Hampton Inn (573)336-3355; Microtel Inn & Suites (573)336-7705 or 1-888-771-7171; and the Alpine Haus (573)336-3424.

The Roy Laughlin Memorial Park at Roubidoux Spring provides streamside tables and grills. The city park has pavilions and privies in addition to tables and grills. Campers can find hot showers and RV hookups at the Roubidoux Springs Campground on the creek's west bank just below the Business Loop 44 bridge downtown.

Dine in Waynesville at Smitty's Restaurant and Deli, the Westside Cafe, McDonald's, Subway or the Paradise Deli. St. Robert offers every kind of dining imaginable.

You'll find the trout-holding portion of Roubidoux Creek on the Waynesville 7.5-minute quadrangle map.

White Ribbon Waters

CAPPS CREEK, Barry and Newton Counties.

From its junction with Highway 97 south of Pierce City, take Highway 60 west four miles, turn south onto Wallaby Road at the Heritage Oak Flooring plant, go 1.7 miles, then turn left and go another three-quarters of a mile to Jolly Mill Park. The restored grist mill and surrounding grounds provide an attractive setting for this stretch of Capps Creek.

Above the mill dam lies a five-acre, often mossy, lake. Below the dam, the creek is twenty to fifty feet wide with lots of backcasting room. Fishing for rainbows and a few browns extends upstream to Hawkins Springs and downstream almost two miles to Shoal Creek.

The nearest lodging is in Monett. Stay at the Days Inn (417)235-8039; Hartland Lodge (417)235-4000; Super 8 Motel (417)236-9200; or J & T Econo Motel (417)235-8329. RV campers can stay at the Highway 60 RV Park on Highway 60 just shy of two miles west of the Wallaby Road intersection (417)476-2116. Jolly Mill Park has picnic tables and grills, but no camping.

Monett has two dozen restaurants, Granby and Pierce City each have five. To the west at Newtonia, try the Country Mart Cafe on Highway 86 a mile west of town.

The Pierce City 7.5-minute quadrangle map shows this lovely piece of trout water.

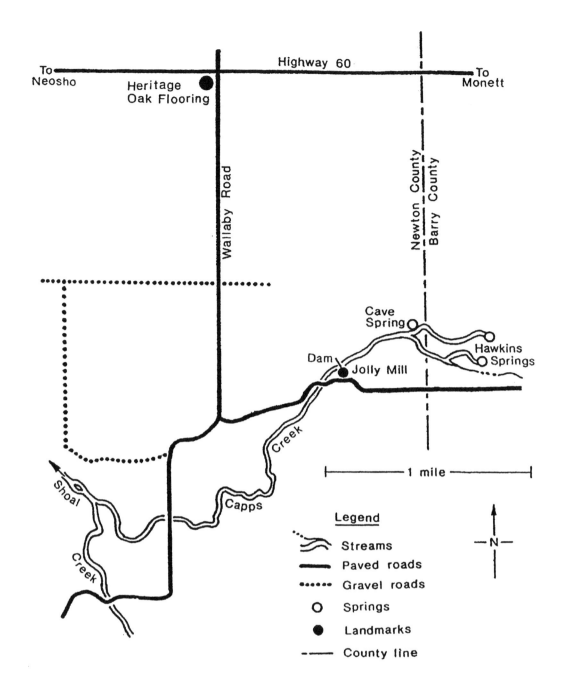

To
Neosho

Highway 60

To
Monett

Heritage
Oak Flooring

Wallaby Road

Newton County
Barry County

Cave
Spring

Hawkins
Springs

Dam
Jolly Mill

Creek

Shoal

Capps

1 mile

Creek

Legend

Streams
Paved roads
Gravel roads
○ Springs
● Landmarks
─ ─ County line

N

CURRENT RIVER, Shannon County.
   Like the blue-ribbon water upstream, this stretch of the Current
also is administered by the National Park Service as part of the Ozark
National Scenic Riverways. It starts at the Cedargrove Access and
goes eight miles downstream to Akers Ferry. It's good fishing for
rainbow trout, especially below Welch Spring, where there are a few
streambred fish in addition to the stockers. Access is limited to
Cedargrove, Welch Spring and Akers Ferry, so you'll need a canoe to
reach much of this water. It's sometimes bank-to-bank canoes in the
summer.

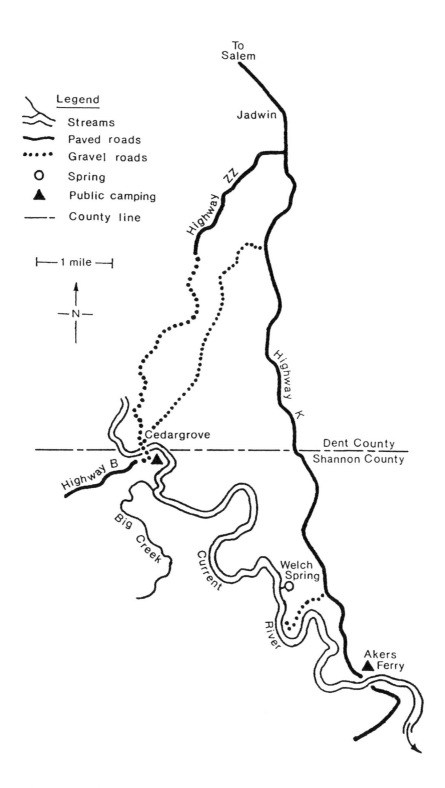

To get here, go three miles south of Salem on Highway 19, then west on Highway K for eleven miles to the junction with Highway ZZ. Follow ZZ for 5½ miles to the upper end at Cedargrove. Continue on Highway K for another nine miles to the lower end at Akers Ferry. Turn off Highway K 1-3/4 miles north of Akers Ferry to reach Welch Spring.

Refer to the writeup on Montauk State Park for lodging and dining information there and in Salem.

There's a developed National Park Service campground at Akers Ferry and a primitive Park Service campground at Cedargrove. Call (573) 323-4236 year 'round for information on both. The Big Rock Candy Mountain Cabins, Camping, Bar & Grill is on Highway B a mile west of Cedargrove (417)932-6917, and the Whispering Pines Trail Ride offers camping two miles north of Cedargrove (573)729-7591. The Akers Ferry Canoe Rental offers cabins and camping, too. Call (573)858-3224 or 1-800-365-AKERS. Jason Place Campground is on Highway KK two miles east of Akers Ferry. Phone (573)858-3228 or 1-800-365-2537. Larimore's Hard Rock Campground & General Store is there, too. Call (573) 858-3345 or 1-800-297-3345. A little farther away at Jadwin, try the Jadwin Canoe Rental's campground at (573)729-5229 or 1-800-937-4837. Akers Ferry, Jason Place and Larimore's also offer cabins, and you can rent a spacious trailer at Barton's Lodging near Jadwin (573)729-5197.

The nearest restaurant to Cedargrove is at Big Rock Candy Mountain. The nearest meal to the lower end is at the Jason Place Campground. Campers and cabin renters can find groceries at Akers Ferry, Jason Place, Larimore's and the Jadwin Canoe Rental.

Rent canoes at the Akers Ferry Canoe Rental, Jadwin Canoe Rental, Jason Place Campground, Larimore's Hard Rock Campground or the Silver Arrow Canoe Rental on Highway 19 (573)729-5770 or 1-800-333-6040. All of the canoe rentals are heavily booked during the summer, so make reservations well in advance.

You'll find this section of the Current River on the Cedargrove and Lewis Hollow 7.5-minute quadrangle maps.

ELEVEN POINT RIVER, Oregon County.

Below the blue ribbon-management water, fourteen miles of the Eleven Point from Turner Mill down to Highway 160 at Riverton are heavily stocked and managed under regulations allowing four trout per day of any size caught on any kind of terminal tackle. Rainbows grow to ten pounds in these icy waters.

Vehicular access is at Turner Mill on both sides of the river, the McDowell Access southwest of Wilderness, the end of the Whitten Church Road, Boze Mill Spring and Riverton.

Nearby motels include the Motel 60 (573)325-4416 or 4727 and the Rusty Nail Motel (573)325-4223, both in Winona, and the Alton Motel in Alton (417)778-6208.

The Forest Service's Greer Crossing Campground at the Highway 19 bridge has pads, tables, grills, drinking water and toilets. Hufstedler's Canoe Rental at Riverton has complete facilities for tent and RV camping. Call (417)256-7161. Richards' Canoe Rental and Campground at Greer has cabins and sleeping rooms in addition to tent and RV camping. Call there at (417)778-6186.

Dine in Winona at Linda's Cafe or Flossie's Apple Barrel. In Alton, try Benita's Cafe, Thompson's Restaurant, Taylor's Pizza or Grandma's Kitchen.

Rent a canoe at Hufstedler's Canoe Rental at Riverton; the Eleven Point Canoe Rental at Alton (417)778-6497; or Richards' Canoe Rental and Campground at Greer.

This white-ribbon portion of the Eleven Point River is found on the Wilderness and Riverton 7.5-minute quadrangle maps.

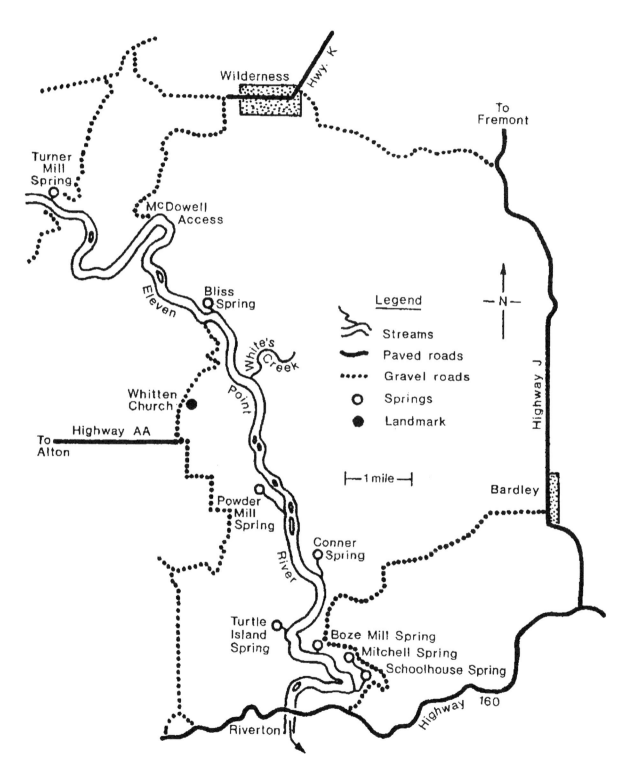

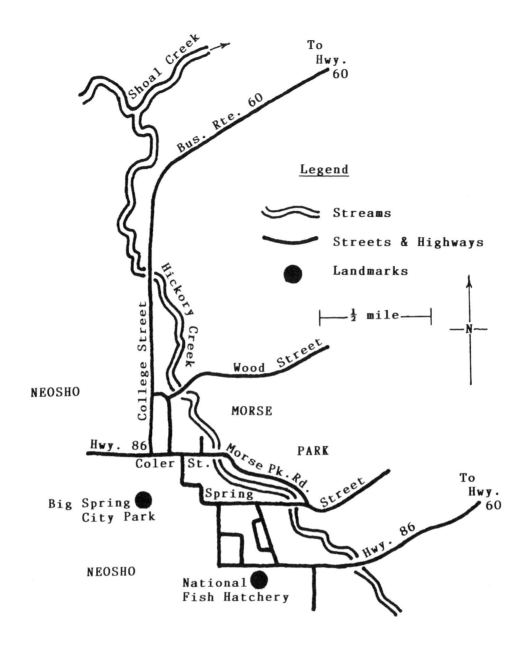

HICKORY CREEK, Newton County.
    Hickory Creek on the east side of Neosho is the newest addition to
Missouri's white-ribbon trout waters. Fishing extends from Highway
86 down to the creek's mouth at Shoal Creek. Morse (city) Park lies
along a lengthy stretch of the east bank.
    For nearby lodging, try the Booneslick Lodge (417)455-0888; Neosho
Inn (417)451-6500 or 1-800-972-1999; Super 8 Motel (417)455-1888 or
1-800-800-8000; Best Western Big Spring Lodge (417)455-2300 or
1-877-345-9645; Executive Inn (417)451-3784; Flower Box Motel
(417)451-7120; Plymouth Rock Motel (417)451-1428; or the Neosho Old
Jaeger Winery and Bed & Breakfast (417)451-WINE.
    Neosho offers two dozen places to dine.
    You'll find Hickory Creek on the Granby and Neosho East 7.5-minute
quadrangle maps.

LITTLE PINEY CREEK, Phelps County.
  Below the blue-ribbon water upstream, 3-3/4 miles of the Little
Piney from the Milldam Hollow Access down to County Road 7360 (the
Old Newburg Road) are managed under white-ribbon regulations. Rain-
bows are stocked six or more times per year, although never during
July and August because the water's too warm. There's no length limit
on the 'bows, the daily creel limit is four, and any kind of fly, lure
or bait is legal. The lower end of this water also holds fair num-
bers of smallmouths.
  The nearest lodging is on the western side of Rolla. Check the Mill
Creek writeup for information there. The nearest meal is at PD's
Cookin' From Scratch at the BP service station at the Interstate 44
exit 179 in Doolittle.
  This part of Little Piney Creek flows across the Kaintuck Hollow,
Rolla, Newburg and Yancy Mills quadrangle maps.

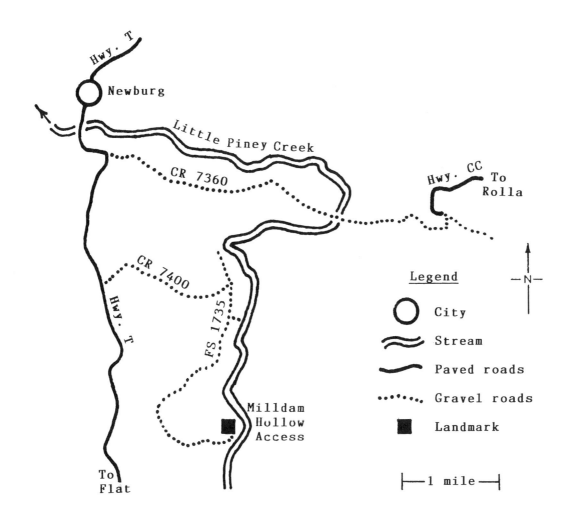

NIANGUA RIVER, Dallas and Laclede Counties.
  Trout fishing begins at the mouth of Bennett Spring Branch in the
state park and extends downstream for about ten miles, although the
first six miles are best. Rainbows and a few browns lurk in water 30
to 100 feet wide, and backcasting room is seldom a problem. Be
careful a passing canoe doesn't intercept your fly during the summer,
though.

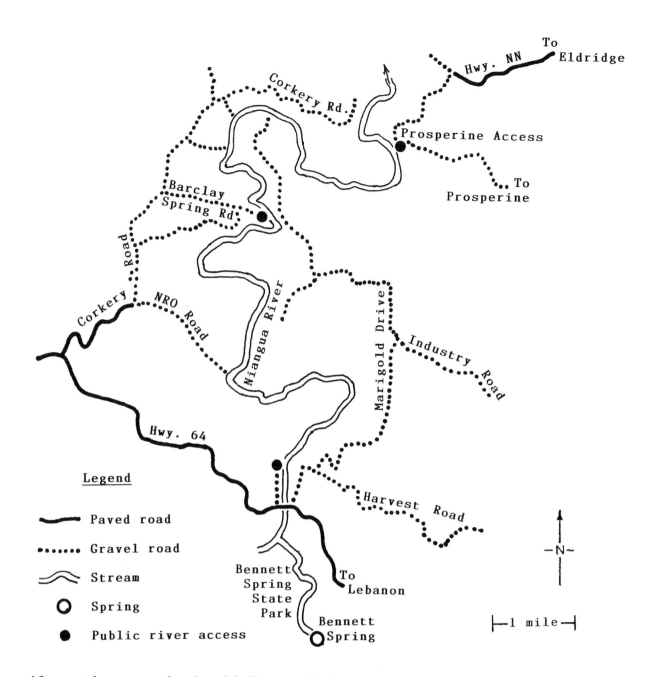

Legend

⎯⎯⎯ Paved road

•••••• Gravel road

〰〰 Stream

○ Spring

● Public river access

Along the east bank off Marigold Drive, access the water at Red-beard's Ranch (417)533-REDS (weekends only); and the Ho-Humm Canoe Rental and Campground (417)588-1908. Get to the Prosperine Access off Highway NN west of Eldridge.

Along the west bank, reach the river at the Conservation Department's large access below the Highway 64 bridge; NRO Campground and Canoe Rental (417)532-6333 or 1-800-748-7249; the Conservation Department's Barclay Spring Access; R & W Canoe Rental (417)588-3358; One-Eyed Willy's Campground; and Maggard's Corkery Campground (417)532-7616. Get to all except the first one off Corkery Road.

For lodging, camping and dining information near the upper end, re-fer to the section on Bennett Spring State Park. At the lower end, reach the Prosperine Access off Highway 5 by taking Highway E west through Eldridge, turning left onto Highway NN four miles to the end

of the blacktop, then turning left again and following the gravel for
1½ miles. To get there from Highway 64, take Highway AA north for
nine miles, turn left onto the gravel at the blacktop's end and go four
miles to the access. There aren't any motels, cabins or restaurants
nearby, but you can camp at the Mountain Creek Campground and Canoe
Rental next to the access. Call there at (417)426-5641.

Because of the river's size, much of it is best reached by canoe. On
the river, rent one from Redbeard's, Ho-Humm, Mountain Creek, NRO, R &
W or Maggard's. Along Highway 64, try the Sand Spring Resort (417)532-
5857 or 1-800-543-3474; Circle J Campground (417)532-4430; Fort Bennett
Tradin' Post (417)588-1391; Riverfront Campground and Canoe Rental
(417)588-3386 or 1-888-67-FRONT; or Adventures Campground (417)588-
7238.

You'll find the trout-holding portion of the Niangua River on the
Bennett Spring, Eldridge West and Leadmine 7.5-minute quadrangle maps.

ROARING RIVER, Barry County.

Three miles of Roaring River between the state park and Table Rock
Lake offer rainbow trout fishing in a wild and beautiful landscape.
Every now and then, a brook trout swims up here from Arkansas, too.

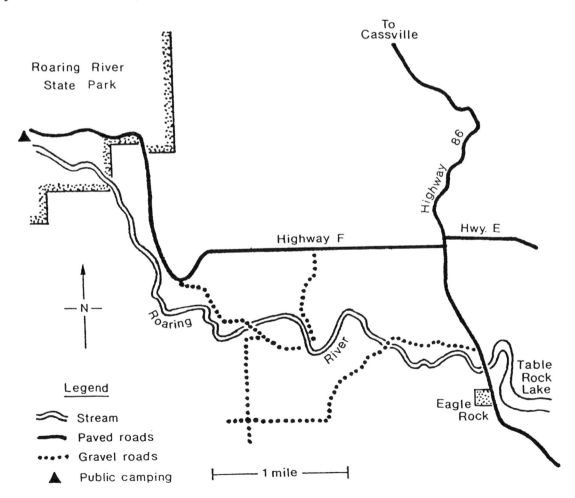

The water varies from ten to forty feet wide, and backcasting room is seldom a problem. There's a little more than the average amount of shallow water to pass by, but the trout are abundant wherever there's adequate habitat.

Check the section on Roaring River State Park for lodging, camping and dining information near the upper end. If you'd rather camp and dine near the river's mouth, Mike's Hideaway Roaring River Campground on the north bank just above the Highway 86 bridge is the only place. Call this full-service facility at (417)271-4215.

You'll find this stretch of Roaring River on the Eagle Rock 7.5-minute quadrangle map.

ROUBIDOUX CREEK, Pulaski County.

The white-ribbon portion of Roubidoux Creek extends from Roubidoux Spring down to the overhead utility line across the creek near the lower end of the city park. It's heavily stocked with rainbow trout,

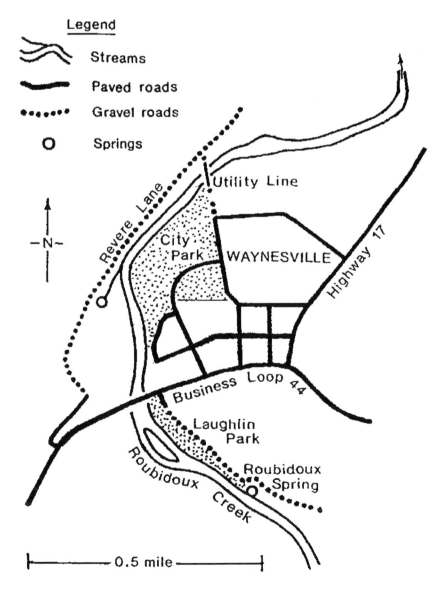

and more than a few browns wander up here from below, too. Because it's right in the heart of Waynesville, the fishing pressure is intense, and most newly stocked fish are taken home in the first few days.

You'll find information on lodging, camping and dining here in the section on the Roubidoux Creek red-ribbon water.

The Waynesville 7.5-minute quadrangle map is where to find this popular piece of trout water.

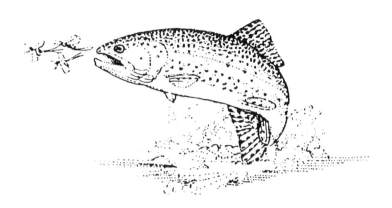

STONE MILL SPRING, Pulaski County.

Stone Mill Spring wells up at the base of a high bluff and flows 900 feet to the Big Piney River. Prior to a recent land exchange, the spring was on Ft. Leonard Wood. Now, it's part of the Mark Twain National Forest.

Access to Stone Mill Spring still is controlled by the Fort, however, and it's a little more awkward than it was before 9/11. Folks without fulltime security clearance must enter through the north (main) gate and show their driver's license, vehicle registration and proof of insurance for clearance.

To find the spring, turn south onto the blacktop three-fourths of a mile west of the Fort's east entrance. Go a little beyond two miles, bearing left where the blacktop forks. Cross the Big Piney and immediately turn left onto gravel. Follow it for eight-tenths of a mile and park.

The spring is a picturesque one-third mile walk on up the road along the river. You'll find flat water twenty to fifty feet wide, too deep to wade, but with lots of backcasting room. Picnic shelters, tables, grills and privies are there, too. Understand, however, that the fish are heavily hammered by military personnel immediately after they're stocked, and the fishing is pretty poor for the next 27 days afterward.

Most of the year, the rules allow four fish of any size in the creel per day, and any kind of fly, lure or bait is legal. From mid-November to mid-February, however, it's strictly catch-and-release with rules identical to those in the trout parks.

Lodging and restaurants nearest the Fort's north (main) entrance are in St. Robert. Check the writeup on Roubidoux Creek's red-ribbon water for details there.

Stone Mill Spring is located on the Big Piney 7.5-minute quadrangle map.

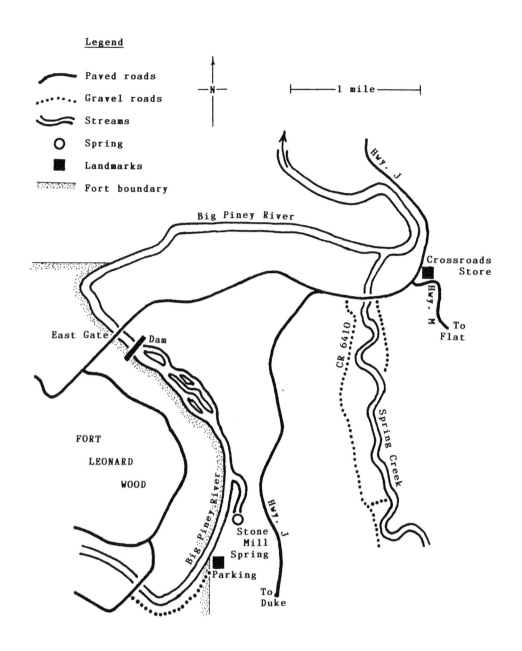

Legend

Paved roads
Gravel roads
Streams
○ Spring
■ Landmarks
Fort boundary

—N—

—— 1 mile ——

Big Piney River

Hwy. J

Crossroads Store

Hwy. M

To Flat

East Gate   Dam

CR 6410

Spring Creek

FORT

LEONARD

WOOD

Big Piney River

Hwy. J

Stone Mill Spring

Parking

To Duke

UPPER BULL SHOALS LAKE, Taney County.
This isn't an official trout-management area, but you can't tell it by the fishing. Rainbows and a few browns come down from Lake Taneycomo, more rainbows swim up from Arkansas, and they all bunch up below Powersite Dam in an area known locally as The Pothole.
This is big water, several hundred feet wide. In the absence of floodwater storage in Bull Shoals Lake and power-generation flows out of Lake Taneycomo, however, much of it is easily wadable. The best wading access is along the south shore between the upper end of the Corps of Engineers' large River Run Public Use Area on Highway 76 and the dam.
Lodge in Forsyth at the Shadow Rock Lodge (417)546-4777; Sand Rock Motel (417)546-5100; Twin Lakes Motel (417)546-3481; or T-Como Motel

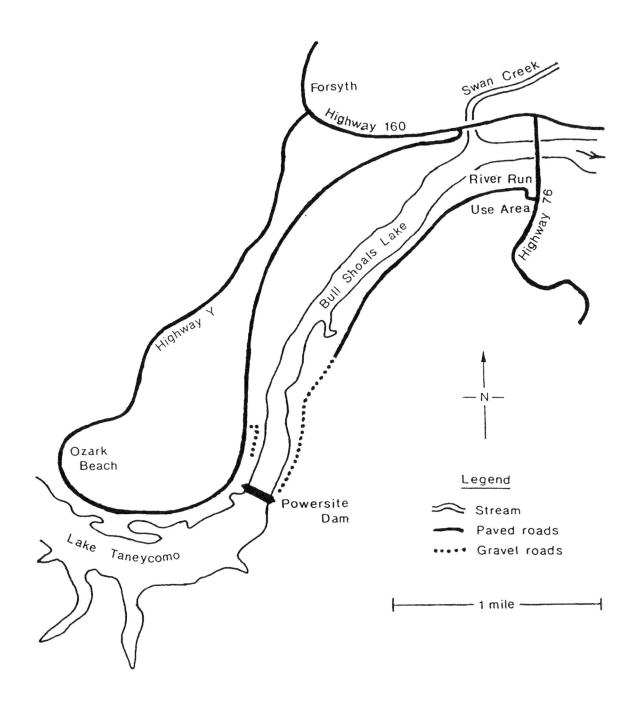

(417)546-3431. Closer to the water, you can rent a cottage at the
Edgewater Beach Resort (417)546-2721.

    Camping and RV facilities are abundant. There's a huge KOA camp-
ground one mile south of the Highway 76 bridge (417)546-5364 or
1-800-562-7560; the Bar-Bee RV Park is just uphill from the River Run
Public Use Area (417)546-4222; Forsyth's Shadow Rock Park is at the
mouth of Swan Creek; and the Corps' River Run Area offers full facilities, too. At last count, there were ten places to eat in Forsyth.

    You'll find this corner of trout-fishing paradise on the Forsyth
7.5-minute quadrangle map.

Lake Taneycomo and Tributaries

If you're really serious about monster browns and rainbows, you'll want to spend a lot of time here.

The first mile or so below Table Rock Dam is 50 to 200 feet wide and more like a river than a lake. You can bank fish or wade much of this water, but you'll need a boat farther down. Always be alert for sudden water rises caused by power generation at the dam, and head for high ground fast when you hear the warning siren.

Public access is at the Conservation Department's Shepherd of the Hills Trout Hatchery on the north shore below Table Rock Dam. Reach it from Highway 165 southwest of Branson. There's also road access on the south shore below the dam.

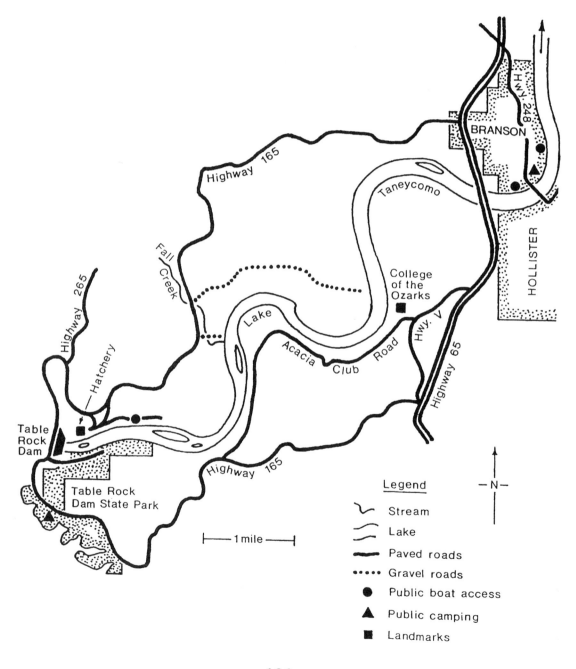

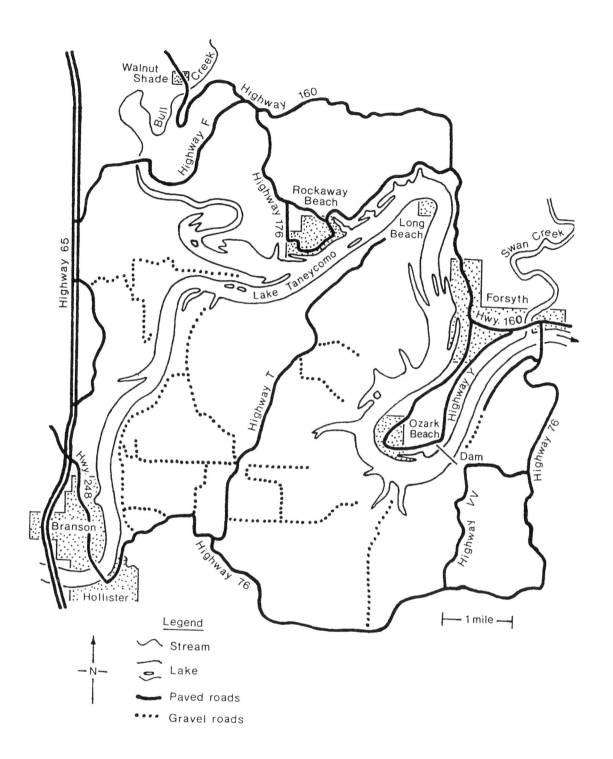

Legend

∿ Stream

◯ Lake

▬ Paved roads

•••• Gravel roads

—N—

⊢— 1 mile —⊣

Throughout the entire lake, the daily creel limit is four trout. Brown trout must be 20 inches or greater in length to go in your creel, and you're only allowed one per day.

Below the mouth of Fall Creek, rainbows of any size may be kept, and any kind of terminal tackle is okay. From Fall Creek up to Table Rock Dam, however, all rainbows between 12 and 20 inches in length must be returned to the water immediately, and terminal tackle is restricted to artificials only. A trout permit is required for everyone upstream

from Highway 65, regardless of whether you're creeling fish or not.
Below Highway 65, a trout permit is required only if you're keeping
some of your catch.

The 2004 phone book lists 218 motels, 75 resorts and 139 restaurants
in Branson, and there are many more in the surrounding communities.
Along the south shore, west of Hollister on Acacia Club Road, rent a
bunk at the Getaway Resort (417)339-0099; Riverlake Resort 1-888-891-
2720 or (417)334-2800; or Trout Hollow Lodge (417)334-2332 or 1-800-
328-1246.

On Highway 165 south of Table Rock Dam, find a bed at the Andrews
Landing RV Park Resort (417)334-5071 or 1-800-678-9780; Parkview Lodge
1-888-727-5883; Table Rock Inn (417)334-4965 or 1-800-234-5890; or
Branson Stagecoach RV Park (417)335-8185.

On Highway 165 north of the dam, stay at the Branson Lodge (417)334-
3105 or 1-800-334-3104; Pointe Royale Resort (417)334-5614 or 1-800-
962-4710; or seemingly countless motels farther east.

Near the mouth of Fall Creek on River Lane, stay at Lilley's Landing
Resort (417)334-6380 or e-mail llresort@branson.net.

For camping, it's hard to beat Table Rock Dam State Park (417)334-
4704.

Dine south of the dam at the Table Rock Inn Restaurant or La Vera-
Cruzana. Doc's Sports Club, the Hillbilly Country Cafe and Pzazz Restaurant & Sports Bar are nearest the dam's northern end.

Lake Taneycomo below Table Rock Dam.

Many of the resorts and campgrounds on the water offer boats, either as part of your reservation or for rent. If you'll want one, inquire when you call for reservations. If you bring your own, there's a Conservation Department launching ramp below the trout hatchery and a city ramp at Branson.

The Branson Chapter of Trout Unlimited honors anglers who release their trophy-size fish with a handsome certificate and pin. Applications for recognition are on the honor system, and can be obtained at most resorts around the lake. Phil Lilley at Lilley's Landing Resort coordinates the program. Call him at (417)334-6380 for more details. It's a great program deserving your wholehearted support.

The area is served by two excellent fly-fishing shops, both on Highway 165 half a mile north of the dam. Be sure to check out River Run Outfitters (417)332-0460 and Anglers and Archery Outfitters (417)335-4655.

Although there are many guides who work the lake, only a handful know much about fly fishing. If you want a guide, arrange for a good one through River Run Outfitters, Anglers and Archery Outfitters or Lilley's Landing Resort.

You'll find Lake Taneycomo on the Table Rock Dam, Hollister, Branson and Forsyth 7.5-minute quadrangle maps.

Urban Winter Trout Areas

The urban winter trout-fishing program is in a seemingly continual state of flux, with the lakes and rules involved occasionally changing from year to year. For current information in the St. Louis area, call the Conservation Department at (314)821-1571. In the Kansas City area, call the Department at (816)356-2280.

Commercial Fee Fishing Areas

CRYSTAL SPRINGS TROUT FARM, Route 3, Box 3337, Cassville, Missouri 65625. Call here at (417)847-2174.

Crystal Springs is primarily a hatchery operation, but you can fish for rainbows in a very small pond or a large gravel-bottom raceway. If you failed to fill your stringer at Roaring River State Park, this is the place to do it. You must keep what you catch, and the only excuse for not catching supper here is that you forgot to hitch a fly to your tippet.

To get here, take Business Route 37 north from downtown Cassville. Turn right onto Highway Y and go a little over a tenth of a mile, then turn right again onto Partridge Drive and follow it for half a mile. Crystal Springs is open year 'round.

Check the writeup on Roaring River State Park for information about lodging and dining in Cassville.

The Cassville 7.5-minute quadrangle map is where you'll find Crystal Springs.

DOGWOOD CANYON NATURE PARK, HCR 1, Box 506, Lampe, Missouri 65681.
Call here at (417)779-5983.

Dogwood Canyon is Bass Pro Shops' representative in the Missouri
trout-fishing scene. It's elegant, even extravagant, and certainly
pricey. On the other hand, you've got an honest shot at a 15-pound
rainbow, too.

Different sections of Little Indian and Dogwood Canyon Creeks are
reserved for different fishing experiences. You can opt for guided
trophy-trout fishing, unguided catch-and-release, or catch-and-keep.
The number of rods on each section is limited to prevent crowding, so
be sure to call ahead for reservations.

Monster rainbows aren't the only feature here. There's an Orvis
shop, guided tram tours, self-guided walking and bicycle tours, horseback riding, Texas longhorns, elk, bison and a gift shop—something
for every member of the family.

Lodging is in rustic log cabins on-site, or at nationally famous
Big Cedar Lodge only twenty minutes away. Call there at (417)335-
2777. There also are countless other lodging possibilities in the
nearby Table Rock Lake and Lake Taneycomo area.

You'll find this unique trout-fishing experience on Highway 86
south of Lampe and west of Blue Eye on the Lampe 7.5-minute quadrangle
map.

RAINBOW RUN TROUT PARK, 2549 State Highway O, Highlandville, Missouri
65669. Call these nice folks at (417)443-3400.

The best way to describe Rainbow Run is to say that it's utterly
charming. Fishing is for robust rainbows and a few golden rainbows in
two springfed lakes much too large to cast across. The grounds are
neat as a pin, and there's a small hatchery, picnic tables, soft
drinks, a headquarters building and pavilion where you can escape the
rain or snow, and lots of shade on a hot summer day. You can keep
your catch, or catch-and-release for a pricey hourly fee.

To get here, take Highway 160 south from Springfield a mile past
Highlandville, then turn west on Highway O. Go 2½ miles and look on
the right. Except for January, Rainbow Run is open every day of the
year.

If you'd like to stay an extra day, lodge in Ozark at the Super 8
Motel (417)581-8800; Days Inn (417)581-5800; or the Holiday Inn Express (417)485-6688. For camping, follow Highway O on west to the
Hootontown Canoe Rental and Campground at the James River bridge
(417)369-2266.

The nearest place to find a meal (maybe) is Drake's Crossroads Restaurant in downtown Highlandville. The Gateway Cafe at Spokane keeps
longer hours, and is only slightly more distant. Otherwise, there are
at least fifteen places in Nixa.

You'll find this little trout-fishing delight on the Highlandville
7.5-minute quadrangle map at the community of Montague.

RAINBOW TROUT RANCH AND ROCKBRIDGE GUN CLUB, PO Box 100, Rockbridge, Missouri 65741. Dial here at (417)679-3619.

For over fifty years, many have considered the laid-back elegance of Rockbridge to be the Midwest's finest. Fishing is for hefty rainbows stocked daily in a mile of splendid, bluff-lined spring creek. There's water here to challenge the beginner and veteran alike. It's strictly catch-and-keep, however.

There's also a large hatchery, old grist mill, lodge, fine motel units and cabins, sporting-clay and trap ranges, and a widely re- nowned restaurant. You'll find names from all fifty states and many foreign countries in the guest register.

Lodging is often booked far in advance, but don't let that keep you from calling. They're open daily from March 1 through Thanksgiving weekend.

You'll find this Ozark trout-fishing landmark on the Rockbridge 7.5-minute quadrangle map, two miles north of Highway 95 on Highway N in northern Ozark County.

SPRINGRISE AT WESTOVER, 546 Highway BB, Steelville, Missouri 65565. Dial 'em up at (573)743-6284, or find 'em on the web at www.springrise.com.

Some of you may remember this as the old Fishermen's Dude Ranch, but you'd never recognize it now. It's under new ～   nore-pro- gressive management by the same folks who brir   ∩ Farms Trout Stream, and a don't-miss destinatior

To get here, take Highway 8 east from   for five miles, then turn south on Highway BR   ⌐er five miles to its end at the entrance

All told, there's fishing fc   ⌐w browns in two-thirds of a mile of Drv   a mile of four different spring branche⌐   ⌐y feet wide, with lots of backcasting rc   ⌐tat-improvement structures. You car   ⌐or it by the pound, or catch-and-release   The number of rods is limited to preve⌐   to call ahead for reserva- tions. They're   ⌐ Sunday year 'round.

Overnight a'   ⌐-bedroom house with kitchen. Otherwise, c'   ⌐, bunkhouse or RV at Garrison's Re- sort 1½ mil'   ⌐lle on Highway 8, then two miles north on Highway   ⌐10 or 1-800-367-8945; or at the Huzzah Val- ley Resort   ⌐east of Steelville on Highway 8 (573)786-8412 or 8472, or 1-   ⌐4516 from March 1 to November 1. Both resorts also feature fine uining.

! ! ! WHOOPS ! ! ! SpringRise has been sold, and likely will not be open to the public any more.

Look for this marvelous trout-fishing spot on the west side of the Huzzah 7.5-minute quadrangle map.

SPRING VALLEY TROUT RANCH, HC 71, Box 115, Thornfield, Missouri 65762. Call these folks at (417)265-3699, or e-mail 'em at svtrout@tri-lakes.net.

Spring Valley offers a mile of beautiful stream, big rainbows, 22 spotless motel units near streamside, unsurpassed dining and the nicest hosts you'll ever meet.

In addition to keeping your catch and paying by the pound, you also can catch-and-release for a reasonable daily fee. Fishing is reserved for overnight guests only—no drop-in day fishing. If you're tired of the crowding elsewhere, give Spring Valley a try anytime between mid-March and mid-November.

The easiest way to find this fly-fisher's oasis is to travel Highway 5 north from Gainesville or south from Ava, then turn west on Highway Z. Follow it for about ten miles until the blacktop ends, turn right on the gravel for a mile, cross Turkey Creek, then turn right again to the entrance. It's on the east edge of the Thornfield 7.5-minute quadrangle map.

TROUTDALE RANCH, PO Box 198, Gravois Mills, Missouri 65037. Give 'em a call at (573)372-6100.

For folks in central and northern Missouri, and for thousands who vacation around Lake of the Ozarks, this is the nearest trout-fishing opportunity. Although it's primarily a large hatchery operation, two ponds hold big rainbow trout for public must-keep fishing.

To get here, turn off Highway 5 onto Troutdale Road in downtown Gravois Mills, go one-quarter mile to the end of the blacktop at the entrance, then forge straight ahead on Troutdale Lane for another three-quarters of a mile to the office. Soft drinks are available, and you can get out of the sun or snow in the spacious headquarters building. Except for Sundays from November 1 to March 1, Troutdale is open year 'round from 7:30 to 4:30.

If you'd like to spend some extra time here, lodge in Gravois Mills at the Drop Anchor Resort & Motel (573)372-6620; or the Waters Edge Motel (573)372-2201.

Campers can find cabins and full-service tent and RV-camping facilities at the Gravois Creek Campground on Highway 5 two miles north of town. Call there at (573)372-3211 or 1-800-573-2267.

The nearest restaurants are in Gravois Mills. Dine at the Our Place Restaurant, Painted Pony Steakhouse, Three Pigs Bar-B-Q & Grill, The Rustic, Dahl's Chicago Style Subs & Pizza, Lyman's Homestyle Buffet or the Mission Steak House. Several of the latter ones have severely restricted hours and days outside the main tourist season. Campers can get groceries at the Gravois Market.

Troutdale is located on the Gravois Mills 7.5-minute quadrangle map.

TROUT LODGE, 13528 Highway AA, Potosi, Missouri 63664. The telephone number is (314)241-YMCA in the St. Louis area and (573)438-2154 from elsewhere. On the web, find these folks at www.ymcaoftheozarks.org.

Trout Lodge is a large, luxurious, full-service resort operated by the YMCA. In addition to golf, horseback riding, hayrides, boating, sailing, swimming, archery, dancing, murder-mystery packages and lots of other fun stuff, overnight guests can also cast a fly to feisty rainbow trout in two small, immaculately groomed, springfed ponds. You can either keep your catch or release it, and the cost is covered by your daily accommodation charge. Warmwater fishing for bass and panfish also is available in 180-acre Sunnen Lake.

Stay overnight in the lodge's spacious guest rooms, or in family-size cabins in the woods or along the Sunnen Lake waterfront. The dining hall is elegant, and meals for special events can be catered.

To get here, take Highway 8 west for ten miles from Potosi or east 26 miles from Steelville, turn north on Highway AA for two miles, then turn right at the well-marked entrance and follow your nose to the lodge. If you're looking for a wholesome family resort with something for everyone regardless of their varied interests, Trout Lodge may be your kind of place. It's open year 'round.

You'll find Trout Lodge at Camp Lakewood on the Shirley 7.5-minute quadrangle map.

WINDRUSH FARMS TROUT STREAM, 100 WindRush Farms Lane, Cook Station, Missouri 65449. Call 'em up at (573)743-6555, find 'em on the web at WindRush Farms Trout Stream, or e-mail 'em at wndrush@misn.com.

There's nowhere else in Missouri quite like WindRush. Fishing is for spirited rainbows and an occasional brown in Benton Creek, a captivating little stream only five to thirty feet wide, but with an abundance of superb holding water. Two stream reaches are reserved for catch-and-release fishing for a modest daily fee. Elsewhere, you can keep your catch and pay for it by the pound. There also are two lakes full of bluegills, bass and trout, all in a gorgeous natural setting.

To get here, travel Highway 68 south from St. James or north from Salem to its junction with Highway NN. Turn east, follow NN for $3\frac{1}{4}$ miles to the end of the blacktop, then forge straight ahead on the gravel for another two miles, bearing right at each intersection. You'll see the entrance on your right.

Lodging is in two elegantly reconstructed 1840s log cabins and a secluded ranch house, each unit with a kitchenette. Check the Maramec Spring Park section for nearby camping possibilities.

WindRush is open between 7 a.m. and dusk every day except Tuesday from mid-February to mid-December. The number of rods allowed on the water is limited to prevent crowding, so be sure to call ahead for reservations.

You'll find WindRush Farms Trout Stream in the northwest corner of the Cook Station 7.5-minute quadrangle map.

None of the Above

Except where noted, the following streams are privately owned. All hold rainbows, and a few hold browns. Some are hatchery escapees or strays from nearby fee-fishing areas or state trout-management areas. Quite a few are wild, streambred populations.

It's no one's desire that these streams be overrun by hordes of meathunting trespassers, or that landowners' property and privacy be devastated. Therefore, I've chosen not to reveal everything there is to know about all of them. In fact, I've omitted many of the smallest waters entirely. Relax—I don't get to fish most of these areas, either.

If you enjoy tracking down trout in out-of-the-way places from sketchy clues and rumors, you may want to check some of these out. Be courteous to landowners and respect their wishes. You'll meet some mighty nice folks that way, and you might get invited back again.

Barry County
  Flat Creek (Cassville and McDowell 7.5-minute quadrangle maps)
  Little Flat Creek (McDowell 7.5-minute quadrangle map)

Christian County
  Tory Creek (Highlandville 7.5-minute quadrangle map)

Crawford County
  Dry Creek (Below Springrise at Westover; Huzzah 7.5-minute quadrangle map)
  Meramec River (Above Highway 8 and below Scott's Ford; Maramec Spring, Cuba, Indian Springs and Cook Station 7.5-minute quadrangle maps)
  Unnamed spring branch (Cook Station 7.5-minute quadrangle map)
  Whittenburg Creek (Fishing reserved for kids twelve years of age and under within the corporate limits of Steelville; check at Steelville City Hall, (573)775-2815, for details; Steelville 7.5-minute quadrangle map)
  Yadkin Creek (Same as Whittenburg Creek)

Dallas County
  Mill Creek (Leadmine and Macks Creek 7.5-minute quadrangle maps)

Dent County
  Schafer Spring Branch (Part of the Ozark National Scenic Riverways; Cedargrove 7.5-minute quadrangle map)
  Parker Hollow Creek (Same as Schafer Spring Branch)

Douglas County
  Bryant Creek (Brushyknob and Mansfield 7.5-minute quadrangle maps)
  Hunter Creek (Brushyknob and Sweden 7.5-minute quadrangle maps)
  Spring Creek (Gentryville and Rockbridge 7.5-minute quadrangle maps)

Franklin County
  Kratz Spring (Spring Bluff 7.5-minute quadrangle map)

Spring Creek (Same as Kratz Spring)

Lawrence County
  Center Creek (Sarcoxie 7.5-minute quadrangle map)
  Honey Creek (Chesapeake 7.5-minute quadrangle map)
  Spring River (Verona and Mt. Vernon 7.5-minute quadrangle maps)
  Turnback Creek (Billings and Halltown NE 7.5-minute quadrangle maps)

Maries County
  Paydown Spring Branch (Paydown 7.5-minute quadrangle map)

Newton County
  Hickory Creek (Granby and Neosho East 7.5-minute quadrangle maps)
  Lost Creek (Racine 7.5-minute quadrangle map)
  Shoal Creek (Below the mouth of Capps Creek; Pierce City 7.5-minute
    quadrangle map)
  "The Branch" (Neosho East 7.5-minute quadrangle map)

Oregon County
  Eleven Point River and tributary spring branches (Below Highway 160;
    Riverton 7.5-minute quadrangle map)
  Greer Spring Branch (Part of the Eleven Point National Scenic River,
    but closed to fishing; Greer 7.5-minute quadrangle map)
  Spring Creek (Piedmont Hollow 7.5-minute quadrangle map)

Ozark County
  Bryant Creek (Sycamore 7.5-minute quadrangle map)
  Hurricane Creek (Sycamore 7.5-minute quadrangle map)
  Little North Fork River (Thornfield and Wilhoit 7.5-minute quadran-
    gle maps)
  Spring Creek (Rockbridge 7.5-minute quadrangle map)
  Spring Creek (Mostly on the Cloud 9 Ranch where fishing is for mem-
    bers and guests only; Cureall NW 7.5-minute quadrangle map)
  Turkey Creek (Below the Spring Valley Trout Ranch; Thornfield 7.5-
    minute quadrangle map)

Pulaski County
  Big Piney River (At the mouths of Miller and Stone Mill Springs; Big
    Piney 7.5-minute quadrangle map)

Stone County
  James River (At the mouth of Tory Creek; Highlandville 7.5-minute
    quadrangle map)
  Little Indian Creek (Below Highway 86; Lampe 7.5-minute quadrangle
    map)
  Spring Creek (Crane and Hurley 7.5-minute quadrangle maps)
  Tory Creek (Highlandville 7.5-minute quadrangle map)

Taney County
  Lake Taneycomo tributaries (Trout have been sighted in Roark, Fall,
    Bull, Bee and Short Creeks during the winter; Branson and Table
    Rock Dam 7.5-minute quadrangle maps)

Texas County
    Big Piney River (At the mouths of Hazleton and Slabtown Springs;
      Slabtown Spring 7.5-minute quadrangle map)

Washington County
    Mill Creek (Tiff and Mineral Point 7.5-minute quadrangle maps)
    Race Creek (Shirley 7.5-minute quadrangle creek)

Just you, and the river, and the trout, and a dream...

STREAM, SPRING AND LAKE INDEX

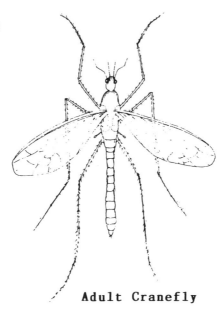

Adult Cranefly

ABOUT THE AUTHOR

CHUCK TRYON was born in post-Depression Chicago but raised in Indiana and seasoned in the trout streams of New York State well before the onset of puberty. Post-adolescence has taken him to the southern Appalachians, Northeast, Lake States and far West in his mindless quest. Now quartered in the Ozarks at Rolla, he's stalked Missouri's trout for nearly forty years.

Long retired from a career as a wildland hydrologist, Chuck's writing has appeared in a variety of books, professional journals, trade publications and outdoor magazines. His natural resource-conservation efforts have earned numerous local, state and national awards.

Chuck is a Life Member of the Federation of Fly Fishers and Trout Unlimited, and also belongs to the Roubidoux Fly Fishers, Ozark Flyfishers and Smallmouth Alliance. This is his seventh book.

ABOUT THE ILLUSTRATOR

TERRY MARTIN was born and reared in Rolla, Missouri, and fell in love with the Ozark outdoors shortly after he learned to walk.

An art graduate from the University of Missouri-Columbia, Terry is now Professor of Art at William Woods College in Fulton. He may be best known to many Missouri anglers for his 1983 Missouri Trout Stamp which featured a streambred, twenty-two-inch female rainbow captured from a spring creek near his boyhood home.

An intense and introspective observer of the natural world, Terry sees wonder in the shapes, colors, textures and moods of Ozark scenes that many of us take for granted. An angler himself, he also scuba dives to study the world from the trout's perspective.

Anyone with eyes to see and a soul to feel will agree that Terry has captured the essence of the Missouri trout- and fly-fishing experience.

RETAILERS AND DISTRIBUTORS:
Wholesale discounts are available on quantity orders:
Contact the author at OZARK MOUNTAIN FLY FISHERS
                                    1 Johnson Street
                                    Rolla, Missouri 65401-3713
                                    Phone (573)364-5509

ART LOVERS:
See more examples of Terry's marvelous artwork at:

              http.terrymartin.net

IMPORTANT STUFF I'VE GOTTA REMEMBER FOREVER